The Welfare State: U.S.A.

An Exploration In and Beyond

the New Economics

Books by Melville J. Ulmer

Economics: Theory and Practice

*Capital in Transportation, Communications,
and Public Utilities*

*The Economic Theory of Cost of Living
Index Numbers*

*The Welfare State: U.S.A. An Exploration
In and Beyond the New Economics*

The Welfare State:
U.S.A. ❧ An

Exploration In and Beyond

the New Economics ❧

MELVILLE J. ULMER

HOUGHTON MIFFLIN COMPANY BOSTON

1969 ❧ Boston

🌿 *First Printing* c

Library of Congress Catalog Card Number: 73–82947
Printed in the United States of America

To my dear friends in Holland,

who helped to provide

a different perspective

Preface

THIS BOOK is focused on the economic problems of the present and the immediate future in the United States. Yet, the basic ideas presented here took root a decade ago while I was in Europe and were worked out over the succeeding years. Absence may have made the heart grow fonder for American institutions, but it also provided a different perspective, encouraging a fresh, and I hope fruitful, look at familiar things.

The particular things that I have in mind, of course, are the leading economic problems that confront us and much of the rest of the world today — inflation, unemployment, taxes, poverty, welfare measures, and the quality of life in a society that grows ever more complex and impersonal. Since they are of concern to all, I have carefully avoided technical jargon and made every effort to write in a way that would be challenging and of interest to all of my thoughtful fellow citizens. The books and documents consulted for this study were extremely numerous — so numerous that the danger arose that nearly every page would be cluttered with footnotes. To avoid this and to make for clearer and smoother reading, I eliminated *all* footnotes; instead, I have provided ample notes to the chapters in the back of the book, where *obiter dicta* as well as full documentation for all facts, figures, and references are given.

Some readers may shrink at the term *welfare state*, but the fact is that Americans have been living in one for more than a generation. I will not anticipate the first chapter by defining it here. But the reader may observe that the welfare state is not something that has been, or can be, turned on or off at will by Democratic or Republican administrations. It survived from Truman to Eisenhower as no doubt it will survive from Johnson to Nixon. This book is written in the hope of contributing to an understanding of the welfare state, and reshaping it so that it will work better.

My thanks go to the Conference Board of Associated Research Councils for the senior lecturer awards I received for the academic years 1958–59 and 1965–66. They provided much of the time required for the research underlying this book as well as the opportunity to exchange ideas with economists and public officials throughout Western Europe, most of whom I would otherwise not have had the chance to meet. I am in debt, too, to the Department of Economics of the University of Maryland for its kind consideration in providing me the further time needed for writing this book. I am also grateful to my friends and colleagues at home, especially Dudley Dillard, Allan G. Gruchy, Walter W. Heller, Lawrence Kegan, Joseph A. Pechman, Charles L. Schultze, Herbert Stein, and others too numerous to list, with whom I have tested

many of the ideas set forth in the following pages. I want
to thank, too, Philip Rich of Houghton Mifflin Company,
who read the manuscript with extraordinary care, and
whose canny eye for detail produced the type of query
that added many hours to my work — but hours that were
always rewarding.

Above all, I must express deep gratitude to my wife,
Naomi. It is not merely that she performed the usual
patient wifely duty of permitting a man to work in peace
— even at home — when he had work to do. She read
every page of this book in manuscript with the eye of a
gifted critic and a saintly discipline that would never
permit substituting kind flattery for even kinder honesty.
I tried to be strictly honest too and do not recall rejecting
even one of her countless keen and helpful suggestions.

MELVILLE J. ULMER

Potomac, Maryland
September, 1969

Contents

The Welfare State: U.S.A.
An Exploration In and Beyond
the New Economics

Chapter 1

What Is a Welfare State?

THE TASK of classifying the ferns, trees, or minerals of the world is an important but usually un-provocative venture. The botanist or geologist — in stark contrast with the economist — can confidently place his specimens in neat, unchanging categories, at least in most instances. He can anticipate interested but placid reactions. A properly accredited authority in his midst can ordinarily call a tree deciduous without eliciting comment, much less an argument. The economist's venture into classification, on the other hand, is seldom so tranquil. Like a shaky dentist, he stands an excellent chance of drilling a nerve — of piercing an exposed center of sensitivity linked to pocketbooks, bank accounts, or passionate political commitments. The task in hand is a first-rate example. The term *welfare state* sparks emotion, excites controversy, and it does so whether it calls to mind Creeping Socialism, Government-With-A-Heart, Rational Planning, or simply a confused conglomeration of giveaways.

Ardent reactions, pro and con, are of course to be expected. The welfare state is a recent mutation in the world of political economies. Born of a peaceful revolution, it has reshaped the basic economic institutions of the Western world in little more than the course of a single generation. It has appeared, with variations on the major theme, in much the same form in all mature democratic nations — from the United States, Canada, Australia, and New Zealand to the mother countries of Western Europe. Everywhere, it altered the seat of economic and political power and, by this fact alone, won the allegiance of some and alienated others. The term welfare state is used in this chapter not to support or deride, but to recognize a transformation that warrants its own subdivision in the classification of political economies.

Grouping all Western economies within a single category, the welfare state, obviously does not imply that they are identical, any more than are all canines, human beings, or democracies. Important differences exist — though these are often exaggerated by mere semantic preferences. For "socialist" in Western Europe, an American should usually read "liberal"; for "economic plan" he should read "budget" or "program for stabilization and growth"; for "state industry" he should read "public authority" or "public enterprise."

The important point is that whatever the differences, real or apparent, they are dwarfed by the more frequent and significant similarities. Welfare states operate upon the same philosophic premise, seek the same general objectives, and use the same means, by and large, to achieve them. Nor was this institutional convergence a matter of accident. At similar stages of economic development, with similar political resources, the Western democracies were confronted over the past three or four decades with common economic problems.

🖈 The Fundamental Premise

Central to the distinctive qualities of this new economic system, which set it apart from other economic systems of the past or present, is the fundamental premise upon which its operations depend. In a welfare state it is assumed that a democratically elected government, *together* with a business system dominated by private enterprise, can and should work *in consonance* to achieve certain economic objectives. Perhaps to a modern ear, the assumption sounds innocuous or even vaguely exhortatory. Yet, particularly when appropriate emphasis is placed on the underlined words, it is laden with content that not so long ago had seemed revolutionary.

Historically, it is but a short jump back to the early 1930's. Up to that point in time, and for a century or two previously, a more or less "pure" capitalism had prevailed throughout the West. In pure capitalism, economic activity and economic decisions were the exclusive province of individuals. Government intervention on the economic scene was practically unknown. In economic affairs, generally, public authorities confined themselves to protecting property and enforcing contracts, except when the captains of industry (more equal, as the saying goes, than other equally free individuals) demanded and got tariffs, special subsidies, or other occasional benefits they considered essential.

Recurrent economic instability, the insecurity of individuals, exploitation of the weak, gross inequities, and
sometimes the ruinous exploitation of natural resources
had always been serious problems of pure capitalism.
Under the crushing impact of the Great Depression, these
problems were thrust to the forefront of national con-
sciousness everywhere. Where prevailing institutions were
already weakened, as in Germany and Spain, they crumbled under the impact. Elsewhere in the West there was
a peaceful revolution. Tentatively and pragmatically, government moved onto the economic scene as innovator,
decision-maker, and regulator — in the United States,
under the pioneering leadership of President Franklin D.
Roosevelt. The objective at no time was to displace private enterprise in its prime job of producing and selling
goods and services for profit. More conservatively, but
still quite radically for the times, the intent was to assert
the public will, through government, to administer the
economy by making the central decisions on economic
matters of collective interest. At the beginning, in the
face of this fundamental alteration in the locus of economic power, business everywhere bristled in opposition.
For the ears of some, amazingly, the polished, aristocratic
diction of FDR acquired a fearsome, proletarian Russian
accent. But gradually the new approach attained famili-
arity and respectability. Democrats and Republicans,
Conservatives and Labourites drew steadily closer on fun-
damentals, aside from details and techniques which are
always at issue. Within two decades the basic political
and economic transition was accomplished, and at least by

the vast majority, the fundamental premise of the welfare state was accepted in nearly every country of the West. Government and private enterprise had learned to function together peacefully, the former being concerned with general guides, aggregative accomplishments, and goals, the latter remaining more or less fully in charge of production and commerce. In effect, the ship of state had been given a rudder.

🎋 *Objectives and Techniques*

Rudders, of course, are useless without directions and directors. Put briefly, the directions, or major goals, of a welfare state are commonly said to be economic balance, economic justice, and economic growth. In the abstract, to be sure, the objectives say little — neither fascist or communist, democrat or anarchist would oppose balance, justice, or growth, *as he sees it*. It is their particular interpretation, and the way in which they are sought in a welfare state, that give them their distinctive content. Here we state the goals in barest summary, merely touching upon topics and problems that shall occupy us in a large part of the remainder of this book.

Economic Balance. Ideally, economic balance denotes a situation in which full employment prevails and inflation is absent. A very large part of government activity in the modern state is directed toward achieving, or at least roughly approximating, this goal. The chief tool employed is fiscal policy, which involves trying to attune the aggregate volume of government expenditures and taxes to a situation of economic balance. An important adjunct is monetary policy, which involves corrective adjustments in the volume of money, credit, and interest rates.

Modern stabilization policies have so far succeeded in warding off giant depressions of the pre-World War II variety. Whether they have come within tolerable distance of the ideal of economic balance is another, and perhaps debatable, matter. Admittedly, inflation has been an almost perpetual, worldwide problem. Recurrent periods of recession, throwing an important segment of the labor force out of jobs, have also persisted. Later on a new plan will be presented here for improving the approach to this elusive goal.

Economic Justice. At least since Socrates men have pondered the meaning of justice and have succeeded in defining it, and redefining it, only in ways that for each time and place can win a tolerable consensus. The situation seems to be no different when we speak, more narrowly, of *economic* justice. In the philosophy of the older laissez-faire, or pure, capitalism, it was held that impersonal market forces, guided by the "invisible hand," would somehow reward the virtuous and punish the indolent or sinful. In effect, people would be compensated according to their contributions to the nation's total output — that is, to the economic welfare of all. This idea has not been discarded, but it has been amplified far beyond the simplistic interpretation of nineteenth-century liberals, and it has also been powerfully modified.

In the first place, it was recognized that in pure capitalism many large incomes accrued to some, not because of any particular contributions, but because of extraordinary or unfair privileges, because of a ruthless exercise of power, or because of inherited wealth or other accidents of birth or history. Furthermore, it was observed that initial success in economic affairs tended to be unfairly cumulative in that success bred success, conferring upon its beneficiaries and their offspring inequitable advantages in the pursuit of additional economic rewards.

Totally aside from the fact of uneven advantages were other difficulties that in practice have had force in shaping policies in the welfare states. A great depression, or even a small one, may throw millions of efficient and guiltless people out of work, and may also ruin thousands of efcient and conscientiously run businesses. So may unpredictable technological changes and shifts in consumer tastes or in patterns of international trade. In short, capricious social tides and currents exact severe penalties from some (and confer benefits, sometimes, on others) that are totally out of line with their willingness and ability to contribute to the nation's work and output. Finally, there are the economically weak — the aged, the disabled, and those who are otherwise physically or mentally limited. If left on their own to the mercies of "impersonal" market forces, as they often were in pure capitalism, they would succumb, jungle fashion, to the mass struggle from which only the commercially fittest survive.

In the light of the above, what do considerations of justice dictate? Here we confront the entire imposing network of social security laws, minimum wages, high and progressive taxes, public housing projects, selective subsidies, and welfare assistance that are the best-known attributes of the welfare state. How effectively they operate and what might properly be added or subtracted are obviously questions of heated, and perhaps endless, controversy. At the present juncture we shall confine ourselves to observing that whatever the techniques, in the United States or other welfare states, the general objectives are everywhere the same: (1) to guard against economic risks such as cyclical unemployment, technological unemployment, impaired health, indigence in old age, or loss of savings in bank failures, (2) to provide a floor for the incomes of economic casualties such as the disabled, widows, and orphans, and (3) to limit, somewhat, the gross disparities between rich and poor.

The fervor with which the last objective is pursued is often exaggerated much to the consternation of those concerned with incentives, industry, and frugality. However, most Americans, and others too, can still summon a sympathetic smile for the philosophy of the old vaudeville sage, Joe E. Lewis. "After all," he remarked, "it takes a lot of money to become a millionaire. A bum can be broke without a cent." The responsive chord, particularly in the powerful middle class of all welfare states, insures that incentives are not likely to be brutally stifled. In any event, current data in the United States and elsewhere show that the rewards for talent and industry, even after taxes, are far from niggardly.

Economic Growth. Crudely interpreted, economic growth means an increase in production over the long run at a pace faster than population, so that the general level of living can rise. The crude interpretation is adequate, and even desperately important, for the underdeveloped countries. In these areas of poverty, progress of any kind must rest first and foremost on the achievement of greater gross production. In the affluent societies that comprise the welfare states, a much broader interpretation is required. Increases in aggregate output per capita — growth in its crude sense — is of course welcomed, but public concern has been drawn more and more to the directions, or the quality, of growth, rather than its mere gross magnitude.

When applied to the developed countries, the interpretation of economic growth, as a goal of policy, takes on a broader meaning close to that of *social progress.* The provision of more and better education, of health facilities, of safer highways and cars, of recreational facilities and institutes for the arts — these are not strictly commensurate with more refrigerators, more color TV sets, and more sports cars. The welfare states, at present, are merely groping with this problem of the quality of life, as opposed to the indiscriminate accumulation of things. Nevertheless, the deliberate attempt to deal with the problem, through the use of public funds and the exercise of public regulation, is one of the attributes of the welfare state.

Communism, Socialism, Capitalism, and the Welfare State

Partisans of the welfare state over the world have been attacked from the left as well as the right. From one side the claim is made that the welfare state is indistinguishable from socialism. From the other side, it is sometimes viewed as just Old Lady Capitalism under a coating of rouge, mascara, and eyebrow pencil. Add to this the helpful statement of a famous Kremlinologist that in capitalism, man exploits man; in communism, it's the other way around.

It is pointless, of course, to quibble about definitions, but the earmark of socialism, since Karl Marx, has been its emphasis upon public ownership of the means of production. Typically, in socialist theory, ownership and operation of productive facilities by the state was considered the *sine qua non* of true economic progress and justice. Yet, in *none* of the welfare states is public ownership a dominant factor, nor has there been any serious proposal to make it so. Specifically, in Great Britain about 80 percent of total production is generated by private enterprise and in the other welfare states the corresponding ratio ranges from 90 to about 98 percent. The industries that are publicly operated are for the most part the inherently monopolistic "public utilities," which in the United States are more commonly placed under public regulation. On these grounds it would seem both misleading and wrong to classify the welfare states as socialist; the term might better be reserved for the communist countries, where practically all production has been collectivized.

At the other extreme from socialism is what has been termed pure or laissez-faire capitalism. Its leading characteristic, as it appeared in theory and in practice (during the nineteenth century and the early part of the twentieth), was that practically all the means of production were privately owned. But this it had in common with Hitler's Germany, Mussolini's Italy, and Franco's Spain. Its other chief characteristics were a democratic government and the guiding principle that in economic affairs the individual decisions of business firms and consumers were to be given free rein, undistorted by public intervention. It is in the latter respect that modern capitalism — the welfare state — differs dramatically. The range of individual decisions has been deliberately narrowed and limited. The role of market forces has been consciously circumscribed. In the achievement of some social objectives, such as a stable overall level of economic activity, the collective will and judgment as expressed through government is dominant. The change is fundamental. It would be intolerably confusing if it were not recognized by a change in name.

Any new economic system, if it is to survive, must win some minimum of economic successes. It will also, almost inevitably, fall into errors that in retrospect may seem obvious and easily avoidable. Even the most starry-eyed advocates of the welfare state must concede that it is far from a utopia. Even the most cynical members of this age of affluent discontent must acknowledge some substantial gains. A society of mixed blessings, as all viable societies are, can progress only if its faults are frankly documented and forthright efforts made to correct them — an objective toward which the present work is directed.

🦋 Chapter 2

The New Economics in Theory

NINETEENTH-CENTURY RADICALS have no particular reputation for prescience, but on at least one important point they were unequivocally right. This was their observation that traditional, laissez-faire capitalism is inherently unstable. Much more remarkable than their recognition of this truth was the bold, unswerving courage with which most orthodox economists of the time resisted it.

The evidence, in retrospect, seems unmistakable. The pattern of business cycles, with their recurring and devastating depressions, was impressed indelibly upon economic history, conspicuously — even grotesquely — upon every record of man's activities from employment, production, and business failures to the number of births and suicides. The testimony is long and conclusive, beginning at the historical home of modern industrial capitalism — England in the late eighteenth century — and continuing through the nineteenth century with broader and deeper economic convulsions leading, finally, to the climax of the 1930's, when the greatest depression of all was felt with awesome power around the world. It was not until the latter event that the majority of politicians, and the majority of professional economists, were induced to accept the truth of the radical view.

The view was accepted, however, with a big difference in implication. Nineteenth-century radicals, led by Karl Marx, had claimed that crises and depressions would ultimately bring about the collapse and final demise of capitalism. Now, in the 1930's, the idea was afloat that government could consciously and effectively intervene in the economic process, restore and maintain stability, and at the same time shore up and preserve the more important institutions of capitalism that had already begun to totter. Numerous prescriptions designed for this purpose were tried and tested from country to country, but they all converged, finally and fundamentally, upon the theory and fiscal techniques attributed to Lord John Maynard Keynes. Today, Keynesian doctrine is incorporated as a matter of course in the apparatus of the welfare state and constitutes an important part of the theoretical background against which all stabilization policies are formulated. In the glamorous early years of the John F. Kennedy administration, the theory won the name of the "New" Economics, although even then it had been around for three decades and had been employed more or less everywhere in the West since the days of FDR. Its accomplishments, as we shall see, are real and important. So, unfortunately, are its shortcomings. Keynesian theory is a salient and enduring contribution to the problem of economic instability, but it has not proved capable, by itself, of providing a satisfactory solution.

♨ The Flow of Spending

In broad outline, the Keynesian theory of economic balance is exceedingly simple. It begins with the observation that spending, up to a point, induces production and employment. This becomes perfectly obvious when it is realized that a business concern will continue to produce only if its goods are sold. To be sure, at times a firm may produce simply in order to build up its inventory; technically, economists think of this firm as purchasing its own output for investment. But any businessman who "invested" this way for very long would inevitably wind up bankrupt. Generally, production follows sales, and the net volume of sales during the year is called the national income.

This concept of the national income is of signal importance in modern economic theory and is worth expanding a bit further. Statistically, the national income measures three different things, all of which, of course, are necessarily always equal. First of all, it measures the total value of the nation's net output of goods and services. (The word "net" here is technical and signifies, in brief, that the value of each good produced during the year is counted in the total only once.)

Secondly, the national income measures the total flow of spending. This is identical with net output, since all the goods produced must have been sold to someone — either to households for consumption, to business itself for investment, or to government for what may be termed "collective" consumption and investment. Thirdly, since every dollar spent is also received, directly or indirectly, the national income measures the sum total of all income payments — wages and salaries, profits, commissions, rents, and royalties.

There are three concepts, then, all embraced by the term, national income — the net value of output, the flow of spending, and the volume of income. Of these three, the strategic one is spending, because it is expansions or contractions in the size of this flow which result in corresponding fluctuations in income and output, and also in employment.

Sources of Instability

The second important element of Keynesian theory is concerned with an explanation of why the flow of spending fluctuates. Orthodox theory, until it was transformed by the Keynesian contribution, was unable to explain these fluctuations. It was this inability that made older economists so intransigent in their quarrels with the "radicals" of their time. For in the older framework of economic theory, market forces tended to keep the economy at full employment automatically. For example, if households saved more (and, therefore, spent less on consumer goods), the surplus of saving was expected to lower the interest rate. The lower interest rate was expected to induce business to expand investment. The increased investment, in turn, was expected to compensate for the reduced consumption, thereby supporting output and employment.

Given such marvelous, smoothly functioning, and self-correcting adjustments, capitalism abhorred unemployment about as much as nature abhors a vacuum. The theory of perpetual full employment — of men as well as other resources — was considered so impressive that it was enshrined as "Say's Law," after the early nineteenth-century French economist, Jean Baptiste Say, who first spelled it out.

There remained, of course, the embarrassing discrepancy between theory and fact. Between 1870 and 1929 there were no less than sixteen depressions according to the leading authority in the field, the National Bureau of Economic Research. Each is traced unmistakably in history by records of the millions of unemployed, the collapse of sales and output, and thousands of bankruptcies. Some of them, such as the panics of the 1870's and the 1890's, lasted years and were worldwide. No matter how orthodox, the ranking pre-Keynesian economists could not ignore these dramatic chapters of history. Nor did they. By a Herculean effort, however, they did manage to remove them from the purview of economic analysis. Depressions, they held, were attributable to elements *outside,* or even opposed to, the business system, such as wars, the stupidity of government officials in charge of money and banking, and the shortsighted gluttony of labor unions. Some analysts with a statistical orientation even found responsibility in sunspots, which appear to accumulate in cycles, and which, they contended, influenced weather, agricultural output, and also the temperaments of buyers and sellers.

The lesson was clear, at least to the established economists of the pre-Keynesian era. The economy, their theory showed, is inherently stable and contains a remarkable capacity for readjustment, for restoring full employment once it is disturbed. The government should do nothing except, where possible, minimize the disturbances. Perhaps it might curtail the "monopolistic" practices of labor unions — or in plainer language, break them. It was expected, of course, that government would do all in its power to avoid war. Beyond this, government could help most by acting least — by not meddling in money matters or in anything else that has to do with business. A deliberate effort by government to intervene, say by providing public works for the unemployed, would in their judgment only make matters worse. Public works would raise business costs by bringing pressure on wages and perhaps, also, by lifting taxes. This would reduce profits and discourage investment. Hence, public works would retard, or even reverse, the automatic tendencies for adjustment and recovery that reside in the business system. So reasoned most of the ranking academic economists, at least until the advent of Keynes.

Keynesian theory differed with their view sharply, both in the diagnosis and in the prescription. In place of self-correcting, automatic adjustments tending to keep the economy equably at full employment, Keynes found constant, often cumulative, forces making for instability — severe unemployment at times, perhaps, lively inflation at others, but seldom a smooth, evenly balanced level of business activity in which all resources were at work.

These cycles he viewed as inherent in the business system with its ever-changing profit horizons, its built-in mechanism for transforming mass optimism into mass pessimism and then back again, always with profound impact on investment, saving, the national income, employment, prices, and output. Indeed, full employment with stable prices was destined to be a short-lived rarity in an unguided, rudderless capitalist economy and would materialize, at best, only by the merest chance. Only forceful, vigilant government intervention could replace a norm of recurring depressions and inflations with a norm of full employment and stable growth. This was Keynes' answer to traditionalists, in the most general terms. On what grounds of fact and logic did his position rest?

Saving and investment, Keynes pointed out, are performed by different people, in different sectors of the economy, in response to different motivations, and in magnitudes that may differ widely. It would be only by the sheerest accident that the quantity of funds that savers currently accumulated turned out to be equal to the quantity that business wished to invest. It is just such disparities between saving and investment that cause gyrations in production and employment.

Some have found the above reasoning about as clear as a typical day in London — and yet the reasoning is quite straightforward. What is difficult or confusing, if anything, is the special meaning given to the words saving and investment. In common parlance the distinction between the two is blurred or obscured entirely. In the terminology of economics they are differentiated sharply and stand for acts that may often be completely unrelated.

Saving is defined as that portion of income *not* spent on consumer goods. It is a flow of funds generated in large measure by the households of the nation. It may flow to banks, insurance companies, or the stock market and may be motivated by objectives such as provision of security in old age, accumulation of a nest egg, education of children, plain miserliness, or other reasons. But note that in the first instance, at least, saving is a *deduction* from the flow of spending — consisting as it does of income received that is *not* spent on consumer goods.

Investment, on the other hand, is defined as the creation or purchase of new physical goods — such as factories, machinery, or inventories — that are to be used for further production. The motivation for such purchases is a single one — profit. The performers are business managers, especially the officers of the one thousand or so giant corporations that account for most of the nation's business. Finally, note that investment, in contrast with saving, is an addition to the flow of the nation's spending.

It should be much easier now to see why saving and investment may differ and how such disparities may affect the economy. Whether investment is undertaken depends strictly on the prospects for profit, *not* on the saving that happens to be made currently available. Business may finance investment through current saving, through past, accumulated saving, or through the expansion of bank credit. The reader should note that bank credit, in accord with current law, may be expanded in the United States to an amount equal to roughly five times the size of bank reserves. So business is never limited in its investment to the quantity of money that savers may currently wish to make available. Nor are corporations under any obligation to use the funds that savers currently offer through the purchase of stocks, bonds, or in other ways. If prospects for profits are poor, investment will be contracted and the funds currently saved will remain unused. From these considerations a general rule of the first importance emerges.

When investment tends to expand more rapidly than current saving, the additions to the flow of spending outweigh the deductions from the income stream, and total production and employment increase. For corresponding reasons, whenever investment falls below the amount currently being saved, the flow of spending contracts and total production and employment decline. If by chance the deductions from the spending flow (saving) were just equal to the additions (investment), the national income would remain on a precisely even keel.

Since the amounts currently saved and invested are practically never equal, the national income is always changing, swinging upward or downward. If such fluctuations are gentle, and occur reasonably near the level of full employment, they present no social problem. But prior to World War II, these swings or cycles in business activity were notably brisk rather than gentle and carried the economy on occasion into depressions of disastrously low production and employment, and on others into inflations in which the total level of spending rose well above that required for the employment of all resources.

The key factor in these cycles was usually investment,

and underlying this, the volatile, effervescent prospects for profit, which could and often did change overnight from rosy visions of limitless horizons to the dismal depths of pessimism, and then back again. For these sudden shifts, altering swiftly the level of the whole nation's economic activity, there were no benign, conveniently offsetting adjustments such as orthodox economists had imagined. When sales were declining and unused capacity was abundant, businessmen could not be induced to borrow and invest in the construction of new capacity, no matter how favorable the terms of lending might be made. As it happens, under such circumstances, banks normally became fearfully cautious and kept their interest rates high. Hence, depressions were typically stubborn. It was during booms, when prospects were bright, that business was anxious to borrow and banks were eager to lend. It took no mastermind to discern why booms and depressions each became cumulative, each in turn became stubborn, and each could typically progress to extremes that at times tore at the basic fabric of society. It did, apparently, take a mastermind to devise a system for combating these cycles in economic activity.

🌿 The Keynesian Solution

Yet, in retrospect, what could be more elementary? Keynes proposed that governments should use their enormous fiscal powers to provide a stabilizing rudder for the economy. When the nation's spending is deficient so that unemployment mounts, according to the Keynesian formula, government should do either or both of two things: increase its own spending or reduce taxes on the public. Lowering taxes would of course enable business and households to expand their expenditures. By these means, the nation's total flow of spending could *always* be increased enough to keep all resources employed.

I say *always*, because it is important to understand that the government's power to expand the economy in this way is unlimited. If reducing taxes, somehow, does not increase private spending enough, government can increase its own spending by any required amount. It can build dams, highways, schools, recreational areas, airports, military installations, sewage disposal plants, medical centers, or provide additional services to clean the nation's streams and air, beautify its cities, educate or train its citizens, explore outer space, and so on. There has never been a dearth of useful public projects, or at least of public enterprises such as reaching the moon, that for some reason or another can capture popular support.

Nor does financing such projects present a problem. The government's ability to borrow is in practice unlimited. It can sell bonds to households, business, and the banks. Furthermore, government has the power, in effect, to create its own funds, either by printing money or by borrowing from its own central bank — the Federal Reserve System. Any or all of these means can be, and have been used; and they are quite "sound" in the sense of being noninflationary, when they are employed at the right time and in the right amounts, that is, when there is unemployment and other idle resources, and when the new spending is in amounts just sufficient, but not more, to bring these resources into productive use.

Notice, also, that every dollar spent by the government has a multiple impact. Public outlays for the construction of schools, for example, increase the incomes of builders, plumbers, bricklayers, clerks, and others engaged in these projects. With enlarged incomes, these producers in turn increase their own spending for autos, clothes, TV sets, new housing, and the like. This additional spending increases the incomes of still others — the producers of the autos, clothes, TV sets, and the rest. In fact these secondary effects, these additional rounds of spending, are on the average quite predictable and must be anticipated and allowed for when planning the government's budget.

Yesterday's heresy is often today's orthodoxy, and so it is with the reasoning just described. When a nation's spending is insufficient for full employment, government has the power to correct the deficiency. Virtually all economists and the vast majority of politicians agree with this, and also, when occasion presents, help the nation to act upon it. Just as fully understood is the way in which fiscal measures may be used to combat inflation. When inflation threatens, because total spending *exceeds* that required for full employment, government can reverse the procedures described above. Taxes can be increased, or government outlays can be cut, or both. As these measures reduce the incomes of both business and the nation's households, most families are forced to economize in their own expenditures, which in turn reduces the incomes of still others. The screws can be tightened — through higher taxes and reduced public outlays — as forcefully as appears necessary, until the nation's total spending is at the required level. Hence, in theory, the Keynesian formula is symmetrical, operating with equal effectiveness on the upside and the downside of business activity. In practice, for reasons that will appear, the apparent symmetry is deceptive; checking inflation has proved much more difficult than checking unemployment. Even more disturbing, attempts to stop inflation have often hobbled the effort to maintain full employment, as we shall see. Great as its contribution is, anyone who has lived anywhere in the Western world during the past two decades knows that in practice Keynesian techniques fall far short of the perfection promised in theory.

Naturally, all governments can and do use monetary as well as fiscal measures for stabilization. Through control over bank reserves, government can influence the supply of money and credit available to the nation, and through control over the interest rate it can affect the cost of borrowing. Sometimes, in instances of mild disturbances, these techniques are sufficient to restore equilibrium. Business investment may be stimulated enough by easier credit terms to snap the economy back from a small recession to full employment. Similarly, in an inflationary situation, excessive spending may be effectively dampened by a rise in interest rates and other restrictions on credit. But more often, the disturbances in one direction or the other are much more stubborn. They may not be influenced at all, or at least not perceptibly, by monetary measures no matter how vigorously they are applied. For example, business concerns with idle capacity and declining sales may not be lured into building new facilities even when credit is offered at bargain basement rates in package deals and gift-wrapped. Under such circumstances, the much more potent fiscal policies must be brought into play. The proper monetary and credit conditions must still be maintained, of course, since coordination of the two branches of regulation — fiscal and monetary — is essential. But the former is the critical, powerful weapon.

As hinted above, there are some real and difficult problems encountered in actually maintaining full employment without inflation. If the practice of stabilization were as simple as the theory, every responsible nation would operate smoothly at full employment all the time. Nor would inflation ever be a problem. Yet all welfare states have been constantly and seriously troubled by unemployment and inflation, sometimes alternately and sometimes in combination. Our next task is to see where the trouble lies.

✤ Chapter 3

The New Economics in Practice

MODERN CAPITALISM as embodied in the welfare state probably owes its survival to the New Economics. Certainly, the institutions of democracy and private enterprise are not so inherently hardy that they could have resisted, necessarily, the repeated onslaughts of giant-sized, pre-World War II depressions. Ending such depressions is the towering achievement of the New Economics. The brilliance of the feat, however, should not blind us to the most serious problem, foreshadowed in the previous chapter, that the development of modern stabilization policies has left in its wake. This is the thus far irreconcilable conflict between the goals of achieving full employment and of avoiding inflation. The conflict has dominated economic policies and political controversy in all welfare states since the end of World War II. It is mirrored in a nearly uninterrupted worldwide inflation interspersed with recessions.

According to the theory of the New Economics, of course, no such conflict should exist. When inflation threatens, the Keynesian doctrine says, the central government has an obligation to increase taxes or reduce its own spending, or both, and this should stop the price rise. The opposite measures should be just as effective in checking unemployment. So goes the theory. And yet the facts to the contrary are incontrovertible. Somehow, despite or perhaps because of the New Economics, the period since World War II has been an era of universal inflation, with the advance of the price level simply accelerating or slowing down, but never stopping, in a disconcerting inverse correlation with the amount of unemployment. The rule, as distilled from recent economic history, is simple. The smaller the unemployment, the more intense the inflation. The milder the inflation, the more unemployment. The relationship is evident both within nations as well as in their comparative behavior.

For example, among the nations with the mildest postwar inflations were the United States, Canada, Belgium, and West Germany. These were also the nations with the most severe problems of unemployment, off and on, since the end of World War II. From 1948 to 1968 the price advance in the four countries ranged from 35 to 50 percent — by no means small but still mild compared with elsewhere. Unemployment over this period, in the same countries, averaged between 4.5 and 6 percent of the labor force — some three or four times the rates maintained in most other developed countries.

Among the nations with the most severe postwar inflations (disregarding, of course, the underdeveloped areas) were France, Holland, Great Britain, Sweden, and Norway. Here, price advances during the 1948–1968 period ranged from 100 to 150 percent. The average unemploy-

ment rates, however, were remarkably low, ranging between 1 percent of the labor force to just a little more
than 2 percent, even after allowing for the small upward
adjustments necessary to make the data fully comparable
with those of the United States.

The lesson tentatively suggested by these figures seems
clear. A very high utilization of resources, reflected in
low unemployment rates, was purchased by and large at
the expense of severe inflation. Some moderation in the
advance of prices was purchased at the expense of considerable unemployment. This general conclusion, indicated by the figures above, is reinforced when we examine
events over time in particular countries.

☙ The Stop-Go Economies

Four times during the postwar period business activity
in the United States surged forward with extraordinary
vigor — from 1946 to 1948, from 1950 to 1953, from 1955
to 1957, and from 1964 to 1968. On each occasion the
unemployment rate dropped, from highs ranging between
6 and 8 percent of the labor force to lows of from 2.5 to
4 percent. On each occasion, also, the price level advanced
briskly, reaching rates of 3 or 4 percent per annum. Only
in the periods *between* these expansions, when activity
was sluggish and employment rates high or rising, was the
price level relatively calm. Not that prices typically declined, even in these instances. Only in one recession, that
of 1949, did the consumers' price index go down slightly.
In all other recession years the upward trend of prices

persisted, but at an annual rate of 1 to 1.5 percent instead of the 3 or 4 percent increases characteristic of the more prosperous years.

The fluctuations of the United States economy were of course influenced throughout by government policy. The phases of expansion were commonly promoted by the appropriate encouraging combinations of public spending and taxes. The phases of contraction were typically ones of fiscal and sometimes monetary restraint. Somewhere during the course of each expansion the fear of inflation had become dominant and governmental brakes were applied. Accordingly, the economy veered back and forth over the postwar years in a kind of half-world of substantial, but not disastrous, unemployment coupled with a substantial, but not disastrous, inflation. The growth of the economy was fitful, interrupted as it was by fairly frequent pauses. The pattern seemed virtually certain to continue under the Nixon administration which took office in 1969. Since inflation was deemed the principal economic problem by the new administration, the standard monetary and fiscal policies were pointed promptly toward dampening the pace of business activity. Their expected results, barring unforeseen changes in the Vietnam war situation, were to reduce price advances but increase unemployment, fully in line with the cycles of the past.

Though on a different level, Great Britain's economy followed a roughly similar course, the ups and downs of which finally unseated the Conservative government. In general, the British tolerance for inflation was greater and their unemployment was accordingly less. Prices in Great

Britain rose two-and-one-half times as fast as in the United States during the postwar years; its average unemployment rate, after adjustment for comparability, was less than one-half as large. And yet, particularly in the light of the profound international imbalances it generated, the British tolerance of inflation was not and could not have been unlimited.

Time and again, using the standard fiscal and monetary measures, the Conservative government was able to retard the swift pace of inflation, but only by introducing recession and rising unemployment. In 1952, again in 1958 and 1959, and yet again in 1962 and 1963 the unemployment rate soared (by British standards) from 1 percent or less to 2.5 or 3 percent. Labourites accused Conservatives of administering a "stop-go" economy and largely on this issue won office in 1964. But prices are not subject to party discipline, and under the Labour government they tended to advance just as briskly as they did under the Conservatives. The power of inflation forced Labour's hand until it too cried "Stop!"; in 1966 a governmentally administered "austerity" program was introduced, which slowed the price level and raised unemployment.

West Germany, with its "miracle" of recovery, is a special case, and yet here too the association between unemployment and the price level was unmistakably in line with that elsewhere. The miracle occurred largely in the years 1948 through 1958. One stimulant was the very substantial economic aid, both direct and indirect, provided by the United States. Another was the spectacular influx of skilled and experienced workers fleeing East

Germany. The latter, in particular, kept the labor supply abundant in relation to demand and contained the rise in wages that otherwise might have taken place. Unemployment averaged close to 7 percent during this period, but production surged forward as new workers found jobs, and the advance in the general price level was less than 1 percent per year — virtual stability compared with the rest of the world.

The changeover in subsequent years in West Germany was dramatic. The flow of workers from East Germany was retarded and ultimately stopped entirely with erection of the Wall. Meanwhile, demand and production continued rising. Uninhibited now by a constant abnormal expansion of the labor force, unemployment dropped from 3.5 percent in 1958 to less than 1 percent in 1965. Wages shot forward and the price level skyrocketed, advancing by 28 percent in just seven years. It was an inflationary rate that obviously could not have been sustained much longer, and it was not. In 1966 the government applied the standard fiscal and monetary brakes of the New Economics, with the standard results: the price rise was retarded but unemployment rose. West Germany too had achieved the earmark of the postwar welfare state — a stop-go economy skirting uncertainly between inflation and unemployment. Yet, it must be conceded that because of the specially favorable circumstances already described, plus an extraordinarily docile labor movement, West Germany's economic experience has been less harrowing than most.

In Canada and Belgium, the pattern of events in the

postwar years most closely resembled that in the United States, in that unemployment was relatively high and inflation comparatively small. In Norway, Sweden, France, and Holland the pattern resembled that of Great Britain, with brisker inflation and smaller unemployment. But in all developed countries the twin evils of instability colored economic policy, and in no case, no matter how vigorous the effort, was it found possible to avoid both at the same time. Perhaps, as an excited member of the conservative Chicago school of economics once exclaimed, "If J. M. Keynes were alive today, he'd turn over in his grave!"

🙼 The Reasons for Failure

The fatal flaw in the practice of the New Economics stems from a fundamental error in the theory on which it is based. The underlying notion is that there is an ideal target — full employment without inflation — that can be achieved simply by a proper adjustment in the government's aggregate expenditures and taxes. Yet, as we have seen, the assumption finds no support in experience. At no point in history, even temporarily, was the target achieved in any country where the New Economics was practiced. Neither poor aim nor lack of effort is sufficient to explain failure in all places at all times. Instead, the possibility must be faced that the underlying assumption is wrong. It must now be considered reasonably well established, on the basis of at least twenty years of trial and error in all the welfare states, that there is no ideal situation, of full employment without inflation, that can be

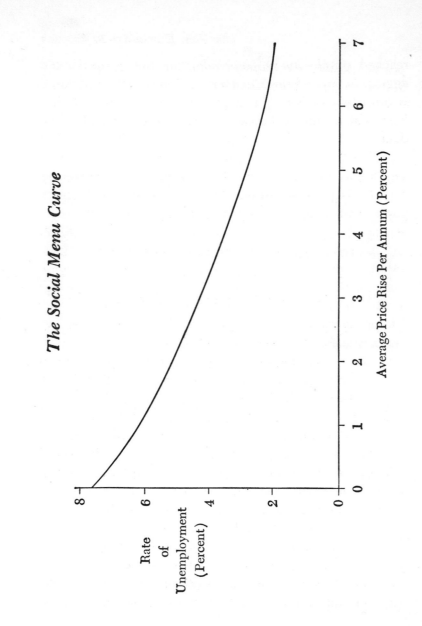

The Social Menu Curve

Rate
of
Unemployment
(Percent)

Average Price Rise Per Annum (Percent)

reached *simply by properly adjusting the government's aggregate expenditures and taxes.*⌉ The latter hypothesis is consistent with the facts cited above, and we shall see later that it can be further verified by analysis of other data.

The Social Menu. This much of the Keynesian theory is true. ⌠It is possible, through appropriate adjustments of government expenditures and taxes, to achieve any level of aggregate demand, within feasible limits, and with it, any desired level of the national income. But the hard lesson of history is that no one of these possible levels of economic activity will be coupled with full employment without inflation⌡ Something seems to be lacking in the internal composition, the internal structure, of the national incomes achieved in this way. The choices actually available, that is, the national incomes that can be achieved, are in every case characterized by more or less inflation, and by more or less unemployment, with the one always varying inversely with the other.

The unfortunate consequence of this situation is that the welfare state is faced with a limited number of unpleasant possibilities, each consisting of various combinations of unemployment and inflation — a social menu of more or less distasteful concoctions from which it is constrained to choose. I have pictured this series of possible choices, roughly as it appeared in the United States in the late 1960's, in the diagram on page 34. The shape and the position of the curve in the quadrant may vary slightly over time, and it surely differs in detail among the various welfare states. But in general form and in economic impact it has been invariable since the end of World War II everywhere among the Western democracies.

The curve illustrates the central point described above. There is a fairly distinct relationship in each country between the level of unemployment maintained and the degree of inflation. The lower the level of unemployment, the faster the inflation. Thus, in the United States it has appeared that even at rates of unemployment in the neighborhood of 7 percent of the labor force, the price level edged forward by about 1 percent each year. As unemployment is reduced to 5 percent, the inflation is lifted to about 2 or 2.5 percent per year. A 4 percent unemployment rate implies an inflation of some 3 or 3.5 percent per year. A 3 percent unemployment rate would be associated with a 5 percent per annum increase in the price level. Getting the unemployment rate down to 2 percent, which has happened only very rarely and fleetingly in the United States, would raise prices by 7 percent per year. Notice that a 7 percent annual increase in prices would cut the real value of a pensioner's income in half in ten years.

The reasons for this perverse relationship, and a method for destroying it so that true stability can be achieved, will be discussed in later chapters. Here, we confront only the ineluctable conclusion: using simply the traditional stabilization tools of the New Economics, full employment without inflation is an eternally elusive mirage. The ideal goal appears nowhere on the social menu of realizable choices. The menu itself must be altered — but this requires tools that go beyond the New Economics.

Fiscal Inflexibility. The standard tools of the New Economics are hobbled by one other fault, not so fundamental and yet serious: their inflexibility. Let us assume for the moment that the social menu just described has been favorably, perhaps miraculously, altered so that one of the choices actually available to standard fiscal policy is that ideal goal of true stability — full employment without inflation. Could we then hit the target, with any tolerable degree of accuracy, using the Keynesian tools of tax rate adjustments or alterations in the volume of government expenditures?

The significance of the assumption we are making may be clarified by stating it in another way. We are supposing, contrary to fact, that there is some ideal goal, A, characterized by full employment without inflation, that can be achieved simply by a proper exercise of fiscal policy. In theory, if the national income headed above A, public expenditures could be cut and/or taxes increased so that the national income would move down from its inflationary height. If the national income tended to fall below A, public outlays could be stepped up and/or taxes reduced, thereby avoiding unemployment. The magic formula of modern fiscal policy would be working, *in theory*. But would it, in practice?

The recent record of fiscal policy in the United States is far from encouraging, despite the fact that during the Kennedy, Johnson, and Nixon administrations circumstances were extraordinarily favorable to its success. By the end of the 1950's all evidence suggests that the bulk of the business community had been finally converted, or resigned, to the doctrine of the New Economics. Leading exponents of the doctrine sat on the President's Council of Economic Advisers. Thus, when President Kennedy took office at the start of 1961, with the economy in recession and fully 7 percent of the labor force unemployed, the setting was emphatically receptive to Keynesian correctives. The nation as a whole, in line with campaign promises, awaited action that would send business activity "moving ahead." Nor was Professor Walter W. Heller, the newly appointed chairman of the Council of Economic Advisers, caught napping. Barely before he had learned the first name of his secretary, he recommended a substantial cut in taxes. The strictly political resistance to a reduction in taxes is not normally considered to be very high. Nor could the recommendation be considered unorthodox, after all the years of public education in deficit financing, beginning with FDR's fireside chats and terminating triumphantly with the introduction of Keynesian economics courses in the nation's schools of business.

Yet, according to Heller's own testimony, it was not until a year after the recommendation had been made that President Kennedy was convinced that a reduction in taxes, as a stabilization device, was justified. Furthermore, it was not until 1963 that the President had sufficient confidence in the move to recommend it to Congress. For its part, the Congress was also circumspect. Not until 1964, a little after the young President's assassination, was a tax reduction finally enacted. Since the effect of such measures is never instantaneous, it was not until 1965 that the tax cut significantly influenced the pace of business activity. Meanwhile, excessive unemployment, bringing personal "depressions" to some 5 million workers and their families, had persisted for fully four years. The great gap between stimulus and response meant that fiscal policy, in performance, had not done the job that was intended.

Even worse, because of this lengthy delay, it is possible that when the tax cut finally came, it arrived at the wrong time. Certainly, as the year 1965 drew to a close, prices were surging forward, the Vietnam war was escalating, and inflation instead of unemployment seemed to be the primary problem, at least as viewed from Washington. From the present writer's viewpoint, the classic pattern of the stop-go economy was in full swing. Professor Heller, by now back at the University of Minnesota, called promptly in newspaper interviews for a tax increase. The Council of Economic Advisers soon echoed the call. After some delay, President Johnson concurred. But on this occasion the resistance of Congress was stubborn. Through 1966, 1967, and 1968, undeterred by any tax increase, prices rose by 10 percent. In mid-1968, about three years late, a tax surcharge was finally enacted, the full impact of which was not expected until 1969. But by early 1969 the momentum of inflation was so great that President Nixon was induced to seek additional measures, such as budget-cutting and monetary restraint, to stop it.

The reaction of Professor Heller and most other New Economists to these fatal delays is that the fault lies with a cumbersome legislative process. Presumably, in their view, Congressmen and sometimes Presidents are either ornery or dense; at any rate they do not promptly see the light, as revealed by the New Economists, and act upon it. There are, of course, other possible explanations, and one in particular that may contain much more of the truth. The thesis presented here is that the standard tools of the New Economics are inherently inflexible, so that they cannot easily be, and ought not to be, changed often and by large amounts. Some other means must be found for controlling aggregate demand.

To give them their due, politicians seem to sense instinctively that tax rates are too important an economic datum to be jiggled frequently and capriciously. Business plans its investments on prospective yields figured *after* taxes. Households of necessity shape their spending, and assume mortgage payments and other commitments, on the basis of their expected incomes *after* taxes. Stability in their accounts would be next to impossible with frequent and unforeseeable changes in the rules of the game. Moving taxes up and down, as Professor Heller once put it, with the "push-button sensitivity" of an office building elevator, would transform the orderly conduct of business and household affairs into a hopeless gamble. Furthermore, tax rates exercise an important influence on the distribution of income and should reflect the considered judgment of the electorate. It is not fitting that they fluctuate moodily with the ever-changing tides of business.

Nor would it be an improvement to place reliance on altering government expenditures rather than taxes. The programs on which the federal government spends almost $200 billion each year require not only legislation, which is always time-consuming, but also forethought, planning, and organization. By their nature they cannot be shifted quickly, nor should they, any more than taxes. Indeed, the volume of public spending, as well as the taxes that finance the projects, ought to be geared to the long-term economic requirements of balanced growth, equity, and a conscious, reasoned decision concerning the division of resources between private goods and public services. Neither the war against poverty nor income taxes should fluctuate from year to year.

And yet, it cannot be emphasized too strongly, the level of aggregate demand must be controlled. Abandonment of the effort would mean reversion to the rudderless, catastrophic economic turmoil of pre-World War II days. What is needed is a flexible, sensitive means for achieving this control to take the place of the present, self-defeating efforts to attain stability by changing tax rates or government expenditures. And required even more urgently, as we have seen, is some device for transforming the social menu curve, so that true stability can become a realistic, attainable goal. We deal with these needs, and attempt to satisfy them, in Chapters 8 and 9.

🖅 Debt and Taxes

Before closing this chapter on the failures of the New Economics, it is necessary to come to grips with a legend — the hardy myth that modern fiscal policy inevitably creates debt, and that debt creates ruinous inflation. The charge is innocuous and irrelevant — more or less like jailing a notorious gangster for burping in public. In the following dialogue, an effort is made to put the myth at rest.

Question: Are stabilization policies responsible, in the main, for the national debt?

Answer: The huge debt of the federal government was incurred much more in financing wars rather than in attaining economic stability. The data of Table 1 show that 90 percent of the total debt of almost $360 billion, outstanding at the end of March 1969, was accumulated during World War I, World War II, and the wars in Korea and Vietnam.

Question: However incurred, isn't the debt as it stands highly inflationary?

Answer: The *level* of the debt, as it stands at any time, has no effect on either inflation or employment. The main effect of the size of the debt is to increase our taxes. Interest payable on the debt at the end of 1968 amounted to about $14 billion annually. This represented about 8 percent of the total war-inflated budget of that year. It is *changes* in the debt, rather than its level, that may at times cause inflation. When the debt rises, it means that the government is paying out more than it is taking in — deficit financing — and this tends to expand the pace of economic activity. If the expansion occurs when resources are already being intensively used, its effect can be very inflationary.

Question: Doesn't it follow, then, that the debt should never be increased?

Course of the Debt of the Federal Government
(Billions of dollars)

World War I

Prewar debt, March 31, 1917	1.3
Highest war debt, August 31, 1919	26.6
Lowest postwar debt, Dec. 31, 1930	16.0

World War II

Debt before Defense Program, June 30, 1940	43.0
Highest war debt, Feb. 28, 1946	279.2
Lowest postwar debt, April 30, 1949	251.5

Korean War

Prewar debt, June 23, 1950	256.6
Highest war debt, July 27, 1953	272.6
Lowest postwar debt, April 26, 1954	269.9

Vietnam War

Prewar debt, Jan. 27, 1964	309.7
Debt on March 31, 1969	359.5

Source: Treasury Department

Answer: No, because when business activity is slow and un-employment threatens to rise, an expansion of aggregate demand, and perhaps an increase in the government debt, may be necessary. If achieving prosperity also brings inflation, even though the nation's total spending is not excessive, then the causes of this inflation must be ferreted out and corrected — a project we shall try our hands at later.

Question: Are you saying, then, that the debt should go on increasing?

Answer: Not at all. A buoyant economy tends to spend money faster than goods can be produced — a trend that is definitely inflationary. The correction for this is to reduce the federal debt. Increasing the debt is necessary only when the economy tends to stagnate. The long-run prospects are for a buoyant economy in the United States, which would make for a gradual decline in the debt, though of course there is no guarantee of this.

Question: Why shouldn't we get rid of the debt once and for all? Why not pay it off?

Answer: There is no need to do so, and if we tried it would be disastrous. Naturally, the government should and does redeem each of its bonds scrupulously as they come due, sometimes raising the funds by selling new bonds. But there is no pressure of any kind to induce the government to wipe the slate clean by calling in all bonds. If the government financed the payoff simply by printing new money, as it could, the effect would be wildly inflationary. If it financed the payoff by raising taxes — assuming that the public would accept so huge a tax boost — the economy would plunge into a terrible depression. Even to attempt to do the job gradually would be depressing and therefore self-defeating, unless it were subordinated to the more important objectives of maintaining stability, prosperity, and growth.

Question: Must we go on, then, with the same huge debt?

Answer: The present obligation of the federal government is truly mountainous, but in the Einsteinian world of economics, where change is ubiquitous, it is not likely to remain so. A personal debt that to Vladimir Horowitz or to Willie Mays might appear enormous would be trifling — barely worth a footnote in a bookkeeper's report — for the Kennedy or Rockefeller families. Twenty years from now, given the 3 to 4 percent minimum annual growth rate normal in the United States, we as a nation will be twice as wealthy as we are today. Relatively speaking, the national debt will be half as great as it is now — provided, of course, that its absolute level hasn't increased in the meantime.

Question: What makes you think its absolute level won't go on increasing?

Answer: Assuming that we can avoid another major war, the answer to this question bears strictly on the alertness of the American public. Despite temporary fluctuations, there is no good economic reason why the national debt, on balance, should go on increasing. But the public must learn to scrutinize the spending plans of public officials at all levels of government — not from the standpoint of unreasoning miserliness, but to insure that outlays are exclusively for goods and services that are needed or clearly desirable. It is a recent pattern of frivolous spending in the public domain, plus benefits to special interests, that threaten to spread contagiously, and it is this pattern, in turn, that could bring undue increases in both the public debt and taxes. The hope for true efficiency in a nation's government lies in the growing economic literacy of its citizens.

⚑ Chapter 4

The Anatomy of Inflation and Unemployment

IN THE UNITED STATES, ironically, we must look to war periods to see how effectively, at least at home, our human resources can be used. During World War II the unemployment rate was pushed down to less than 2 percent of the civilian labor force. The gainfully employed embraced practically everyone able and willing to work including the inexperienced, the unskilled, the elderly, and the disadvantaged. The idle few represented the bare minimum of those likely to be caught between jobs by a statistical survey. Proving that it was no accident, unemployment again dipped to the neighborhood of 2 percent during the Korean War.

In the high-pressure economies of Europe, as we have seen, the 2 percent rate or a bit less is fairly common in boom periods, even after their statistics are adjusted to our own Census Bureau standards. In a special study conducted for Congress in 1959, the Bureau of Labor Statistics conservatively estimated that the minimum unavoidable or "frictional" unemployment in the United States was not greater than 2.5 percent, whether in war or peace.

These observations raise a disturbing question about the

phrase "full employment" as used by many authorities in
the United States. The conventional estimate — adopted
by the Council of Economic Advisers and much of the
academic world throughout the 1960's — is that full employment exists when 4 percent of the labor force is unemployed. But such usage implies that in wartime, and
more frequently in Europe, we must have had "overfull"
employment, an idea that may be puzzling for us simple
souls who have never had a better-than-perfect score in
anything. The question persists: What do these authorities
mean when they say "full employment"? The answer provided by the relevant literature is equivocal. It means the
lowest unemployment rate that can be sustained *without
incurring "too much" inflation.*

Given this definition, the 2 percent unemployment rate
is ruled out as overfull, since during World War II the
price rise was at least 8 percent per annum, too much in
anyone's estimation. But as sights are lowered, judgments
begin to differ. The 4 percent unemployment rate — officially endorsed as full employment under the Kennedy
administration — implies a 3 or 4 percent per year increase
in the price level, as will be recalled from our discussion of
the "social menu." To some conventionally liberal economists (such as Paul A. Samuelson and Robert Solow of
MIT or Walter W. Heller of the University of Minnesota)
this is a tolerable degree of inflation. But the same degree
of inflation is distinctly *not* tolerable to some equally rep-
utable though not quite so "liberal" economists (such as
Arthur F. Burns, the former Columbia economist who became White House adviser to President Nixon, or Paul W.

McCracken, chairman of the Council of Economic Advisers under President Nixon, or Henry C. Wallich of Yale), and of course it is not tolerable to pensioners, teachers, civil servants, unorganized workers, the thrifty who save for their children's education, and the many millions of others who cannot speculate or gamble effectively to offset or even profit by a vigorous advance in prices. The value of a fixed income, in terms of its purchasing power, would be cut in half in less than 18 years if prices rose by 4 percent per annum.

Even more important, despite the official status of the 4 percent unemployment goal, the 3 or 4 percent annual price rise that goes with it has not been treated as tolerable by any government administration in the United States since World War II. Except in wartime, whenever the economy was moved near or touched this level, it has been drawn away as quickly as possible. The result under Democratic and Republican administrations alike has been the stop-go economy already described, with considerably more unemployment but much less inflation, on the average, than the European model. Another result is that we have never even distantly approached in any peacetime year the unemployment rate of 2 percent — which is as good an estimate as any of *true* full employment — that war experience indicates is possible. In other words, even in the best of peacetime years we have had excessive unemployment, with its side effect of poverty, and brisk inflation too. We have shouldered, rich and poor alike, the high taxes necessary to "cure" poverty. It is as though we were being asked to abolish slums by shifting them

all to good neighborhoods, or abolish adultery by for-
bidding marriage. Notice that even the pseudo full employment level — 4 percent unemployment in the nation
as a whole — implies from 7 to 10 percent unemployment
among Negroes and the unskilled.

One elementary step in the right direction is to state the
goals of policy with all possible honesty and accuracy. As
pointed out by a former member of the Council of Economic Advisers, Otto Eckstein of Harvard:

> The Council of Economic Advisers (under Kennedy and
> Johnson) has selected 4.0 percent (unemployment as a goal)
> on the ground that it is consistent with price level stability.
> It does not seem that the full employment objective should
> be defined in terms of its compatibility with another ob-
> jective. Perhaps, with the present structure of the economy,
> full employment is inconsistent with stable prices; perhaps
> not. But it seems to be implicit theorizing to achieve com-
> patibility of the objectives by lowering one's goals until
> compatibility is achieved by definition. If new policies are
> needed to achieve genuine compatibility, let us consider
> them on their own merits.

In short, drawing targets closer in order to make them
easier to hit is not likely to improve marksmanship, either
on the range or in public policy. To jumble the metaphor
further, it is not cricket. If full employment prevails, as
common sense suggests, when all who are able and willing
to work can find jobs, then the statistical description of
that situation would seem fairly obvious. The minimum
unemployment level, that is, the number likely to be "between jobs" even in the best of economic circumstances,

appears to be in the neighborhood of 2 percent. Our objective in this chapter will be to determine *why* stable prices are not at present compatible with this true full employment level, or even with quite distant approaches to it. The foundation will then be laid for the corrective formulations to be presented later.

✿ The Causes of Inflation

Excess Demand. The fact that inflation is a many-faced enemy has led its determined opponents on several occasions to march vigorously in the wrong direction. Its most familiar face, and the one beloved by some newspaper seers, cartoonists, and a large part of the banking community, is overspending. A bloated ogre with cash spilling out of its overstuffed pockets will do as a visual image. It is just because the image is so popularly held, and the ideas associated with it have been so loosely applied, that it has often served to obfuscate rather than clarify the nature of modern inflation. For our purposes we shall have to give "overspending" a precise definition. Any increase in the nation's total spending (or aggregate demand), *after* the point of full employment has been reached, we shall consider as resulting in overspending. The type of inflation incident to this circumstance is commonly called *excess demand* or *demand-pull* inflation by economists. We shall go along with the first of these phrases and, as suggested above, we shall define full employment as implying a 2 percent rate of unemployment.

Two observations, of seminal importance for policy,

follow from this definition. Excess demand inflation, at least since the end of World War II, has never occurred in the United States, although it has appeared from time to time in Western Europe. [In the United States we have consistently dampened our economy well before the full employment level was reached, thereby avoiding excess demand inflation.] The "premature" dampening, of course, was stimulated by the appearance of other types of inflation, described below, which appeared long before the unemployment rate had been reduced to the 2 percent minimum. The second observation is that excess demand inflation is amenable to a relatively simple cure. It is even easier to depress aggregate demand by fiscal measures than it is to expand it. If a rise in aggregate demand above the 2 percent unemployment rate level were our only problem, it could readily be corrected, though no doubt with some lag, by a rise in taxes, a reduction in public spending, or even by a tight control over the growth of the money supply and a rise in interest rates. In short, it is *this* type of inflation — excess demand — that can conceivably be checked by the standard Keynesian tools. Unfortunately, there are other types and other sources of inflation, some of which are much less tractable.

Bottlenecks. Before turning to the malignant, or at least more stubborn, forms of the disease, a second, less dangerous type of inflation must be described. This is the advance in prices that results from "bottlenecks." When aggregate demand rises, even if the economy is at a low level of operation, much depends on *how fast* it is permitted to rise. The overly simple view is that the increase in spending will always be matched by a corresponding rise in production, so long as unemployed resources are available; hence, prices will not rise. Such a neat correspondence of spending and output is possible but not often realized. The reason is that production of all goods and services cannot be expanded at the same rate or with the same ease. There are "bottlenecks" holding back the supply of some things, at least temporarily, so that their expansion takes longer than others. Meanwhile, with the general level of demand increasing, their prices rise. Some of these rising prices — say that of steel or coal — will enter as costs into the production of other things, such as autos or electricity, causing *their* prices to rise in turn. Like any other form of the disease, bottleneck inflation is contagious.

Yet, like the common cold, it is normally short-lived and goes away by itself. Bottlenecks, after all, refer to scarcities that are temporary. After a time it becomes possible to build the new capacity, or sow the fields, or obtain the additional workers to produce more of the goods that were temporarily scarce. Then their prices decline, or at least stop increasing. This kind of inflation, therefore, tends to subside naturally. Moreover, even the initial advance in prices, stemming from bottleneck scarcities, can be largely avoided or tempered by properly moderating the growth rate of aggregate demand.

Structural Inflation and the Pattern of Unemployment. We come now to a more dangerous — perhaps *the* most menacing — form of inflation. It stems from a type of scarcity that becomes so general and so prolonged, as the nation's total spending advances, that the word bottleneck cannot be sensibly applied to it. This is the nationwide scarcity of skilled workers that unfailingly develops at an early stage in a business expansion. It is a scarcity that results in a sharp and persistent price rise for the services of a large part of the working population, while another part of the labor force languishes in unemployment. It is not self-corrective since the skills demanded, typically, are not easily acquired, and because some of the skills — of scientists, other professionals, college-trained technicians, for example — could not be acquired by some of the unemployed even if they were given eternity to do it. Hence, for many types of skilled workers demand soon outstrips supply, the wages, salaries, or fees of these workers rise sharply, and the prices of the goods and services they produce rise too. Since there is no prompt corrective — that is, since the supply of these services *remains* scarce — their prices continue to rise, unless the whole level of aggregate demand drops; and the advance in these wages, salaries, and prices, by direct and indirect routes, permeates the remainder of the economy.

Underlying this phenomenon is an important trend, most pronounced over the past two decades, that in the words of the Census Bureau's manpower expert, Herman P. Miller, consists of the "persistent intrusion of brainpower" rather than brawn in the nation's labor requirements. Another authority, Walter Galenson of the University of California, describes the trend this way:

The Anatomy of Inflation and Unemployment

The entire direction of labor demand emphasizes the increasing importance of education as a qualification for employment. The demand for professionals is growing more rapidly than that for any other occupational group. Teachers, physicians, nurses, scientists, and engineers will be in very short supply for some time to come. Our corps of managers in industry and commerce has been increasing by leaps and bounds, though future growth is expected to be somewhat more moderate than for professionals. Among blue-collar workers, the skilled trades are very much in demand, despite the lack of buoyancy in manual employment as a whole. Many skilled trades require a formal apprenticeship, and for most, a high school degree is a minimum requirement. Even experienced skilled journeymen must go back to school to qualify for work in new industries like atomic energy and aerospace . . . Job content does not remain stable over time, but generally moves in the direction of increased skill requirements, at all levels.

The consequence is that in relation to the potential supply, the demand for workers over the last decade or two has been lopsided. Even when aggregate demand is very low and unemployment distressingly high, as it was in 1961, job opportunities are likely to remain abundant, as any reader of the help wanted ads can verify, for mechanics, electronic and production technicians, draftsmen, computer programmers, secretaries, machinists, nurses, engineers, teachers, accountants, carpenters, mechanical designers, and a variety of other skilled employees. Government statistics make the situation plainer. In the depressed year of 1961 the national unemployment rate was 7 percent, which was bad enough, but for unskilled laborers the unemployment rate was 14 percent and for semiskilled factory workers nearly 10 percent. In that same year the unemployment rates were 2 percent for professional and technical workers, less than 2 percent for business and public administrators, and 6 percent for craftsmen. Naturally, as business improved in subsequent years the scarcity of skilled workers intensified and their wages and salaries advanced spectacularly. In the inflationary year of 1966, with the Vietnam war in full swing, the unemployment rates for highly trained personnel fell close to 1 percent, suggesting that a man who left or lost a job in these trades must have raced for a plane to take another. But for the nation as a whole in that year the unemployment rate was 4 percent and for unskilled industrial workers the rate was 7 percent. In this same year, in which the government's "full employment" goal had been reached, the unemployment rate for Negroes was also 7 percent and for youngsters in the labor force below the age of 20 the rate was considerably more than 10 percent. But notice that most of the unemployed Negroes were unskilled and poorly educated and the youngsters were largely inexperienced school dropouts. Also counting heavily among the unemployed even in good years, besides the unskilled, Negroes, and youths, are older workers displaced by technological change or the contraction of declining industries.

For our immediate purpose, the important point of the foregoing analysis is this. Long before the government's official and modest version of full employment is reached for the nation as a whole, full employment is realized for a large part of the labor force: the well educated and the skilled. The rise in their wages and salaries make a substantial inflation inevitable, even while the national unemployment rate remains high, and as we have seen, sickeningly high for the unskilled and otherwise disadvantaged. For this reason alone, an attempt to get the unskilled in jobs and reach *true* full employment, *simply by expanding aggregate demand,* would induce an inflation so severe that no nation could sustain it for very long. For this reason alone, except in wartime, the United States government has never tried.

Cost-Push and Psychology. There are two other causes of inflation, in practice so entwined that they can hardly be distinguished. One is the persistent upward pressure placed on wages and prices as a result of the high degree of monopoly power achieved by both unions and business corporations in modern industry. This is typically called *cost-push* inflation. The second is the upward pressure on prices resulting from *inflationary psychology* — the mere expectation by people that in virtually all circumstances the price level will definitely rise. The expectation, of course, has been justly considered as reliable as predictions of the biannual equinox. Prices on the average have advanced briskly since the end of World War II and have at no point, even in recessions, evidenced any serious intention to go down. Only a major depression, which both Republican and Democratic administrations have shown their ability and readiness to avert, would knock wages and prices down appreciably. The public knows this and acts accordingly, as we shall now see.

Inflationary psychology gives rise to what may be called the "incomes race." At each and every opportunity income recipients attempt to push up the rate of their emolument, largely because of what they feel is merely sensible self-defense. With the price level expected to rise, a failure to obtain a higher rate of pay, in dollars, would mean an actual loss in purchasing power, a distinct drop in the real level of living. The danger of pricing oneself out of the market is negligible when nearly everybody reacts in the same way. Thus emboldened, people attempt to anticipate inflation, and by so doing insure that the expectation will come to pass.

Viewed in this way, cost-push inflation is just one aspect of inflationary psychology — although it is the one on which policymakers, to their grief, have placed nearly exclusive emphasis. Unions and their leaders unceasingly seek higher rates of pay and/or fringe benefits. Even in recessions and in the presence of considerable unemployment in their own ranks, they successfully resist reductions and sometimes secure additional advances. When these wage increases exceed the pace of productivity, as they often do, price rises become inevitable unless profits are reduced. For their part, corporations are practically never impressed by the need for lower profits and may even, as income recipients, aspire to a larger share in the growing money value of the nation's total produce. Wage increases are normally passed on to the public in price increases, often with an extra fillip. The fear of pricing themselves out of the market, when all other values are rising, leaves them undaunted.

The behavior of organized workers and giant corporations in the big business industries, although highly publicized, is no different in general objective from that of other sectors of the economy. Their pursuit of higher money incomes is duplicated, and sometimes exceeded in ingenuity and determination, by physicians, accountants, engineers, lawyers, scientists, farmers, smaller business concerns, and organized and unorganized workers in other industries. Inflationary psychology, including the cost-push phenomenon, lends a powerful impetus to the price rise which for the "structural" reasons cited earlier would under present circumstances have been in progress anyway.

☙ Direct Price Controls

Perhaps it is needless to repeat that the only effective counteragent for inflation, that any welfare state has discovered during the postwar years, has been the creation of substantial unemployment. Obviously, this is a medicine with side effects at least as serious as the ailment it is meant to cure, and hence it is administered only in modest doses. Often in desperation, however, particularly when inflation upsets the equilibrium of a nation's foreign balances, an effort is made to control prices directly. These efforts have taken two forms, which warrant brief mention.

The General Freeze. By its nature, a freeze of prices or wages or both is a gesture of panic. Changes in prices relative to one another, and changes in wages relative to one another, are essential to the operation of any economy, including the communist nations. It is only through such changes that the basic forces of supply and demand can do their job of determining how much of each good to produce and how resources, including manpower, ought to be allocated among all the alternative uses to which they might be put. When prices and wages are frozen, these tasks remain unattended with the result that meaningless surpluses occur in some markets, pointless scarcities in others, while the allocation of resources grows less efficient with each passing day. Moreover, like a lid on a boiling pot, the price ceiling is inevitably raised here and there, since the basic forces of inflation remain unabated; the government is forced to recognize and admit more and more exceptions to the general rule, and gray and black markets become increasingly common. General freezes, therefore, typically melt in short order. Nevertheless, as a temporary measure, many of the Western nations including France, Great Britain, Belgium, Holland, and Norway have tried this tactic, some of them on more than one occasion. The maximum achieved in any case was to retard the inflation briefly until fiscal and monetary measures were able to take over for a further dampening — or in some instances until the country took the momentous step of a currency devaluation.

Specific Price Controls. At one time or another practically all the welfare states have made an effort to control prices and wages in some detail, not simply with a freeze, but by setting specific maximum prices for at least some particular goods and services. In European countries this has usually been accomplished through formal regulatory procedures based on definite statutory authority. In the United States informal, "voluntary" controls have been tried, particularly by Presidents Kennedy and Johnson.

Whether voluntary or otherwise, the schemes for specific price controls in all welfare states have been patterned along the same lines. Standards — called "guideposts" in the United States — are established, and to these business and labor are asked to adhere. Wages, on the average, are supposed to be kept in line with the average national increase in productivity, usually estimated at somewhat more than 3 percent per annum in the United States. Prices are supposed to be kept in line with unit costs, that is, to costs of production per unit of output. Deviations from the general pattern, in theory, are permitted when warranted by particular circumstances of demand and supply. Unjustified increases in either prices or wages are ruled out — and there, in practice, is the rub. Applying these rules strictly in an inflationary period would require a continuing market study for every good or service in the economy — a virtually impossible task.

For example, a wage increase for steelworkers in excess of the national productivity gain would be justified if the demand for steelworkers (perhaps because of a boom in the sales of machinery, autos, or other steel consuming industries) had increased and higher wages were needed to attract additional men. A price rise for candy would be justified if the import price of sugar had advanced. Investigating such situations with sufficient care to support a price or wage control decision, even for a single industry, would normally require the concentrated attention of a substantial research staff for a few months at least. As just suggested, to study each price and wage in the economy (there are literally millions of them!), meticulously and judiciously, would be physically impossible. Hence, in practice, government administrators have concentrated attention on a relatively few "key" industries, more or less disregarding the rest except for general exhortations and appeals to patriotism. The key industries are commonly interpreted to be the commercially most important ones such as petroleum, steel, autos, or copper, in which giant corporations usually account for most or all of the output and workers are organized in powerful unions.

Toward such key industries, price controllers in all welfare states have been specially, and often exclusively, alert. When a wage boost in excess of the national productivity gain was contracted, a government official would step in demanding a rollback, or a convincing argument in justification. When a price increase was announced or disclosed, again a government official would intervene in an effort to get it canceled. Meanwhile, of course, a host of other incomes and prices were left unattended — prices and wages in the smaller or less-concentrated or presumably less-important industries, the fees of physicians, the wages or salaries or other incomes of unorganized workers, business executives, scientists, barbers, engineers, landlords, accountants, real estate dealers, farmers, bondholders, stock speculators, retailers, lawyers, and others. Those unions and business corporations in the key industries were less than appreciative for being singled out and were quick to charge public administrators with discrimination — an argument that inevitably gathered more weight the longer the government persisted in its practice of "selective" price control.

Moreover, when challenged, the government had no supportable and practical plan for adjudicating the claims and counter claims to shares in the national income of all the different branches of capital, labor, agriculture, and the professions. Even were it determined to try, it had no ready method for acquiring the necessary foundation of mountainous facts nor the generally acceptable standards necessary for elusive questions of equity. Market forces make these decisions continuously, swiftly, and impersonally. Detailed intervention by government raises the specter of a Pandora's box of interminable studies and analyses, each of which will be out of date before completion.

For these and other reasons none of the plans for government price control have lasted very long, and as the data already cited show conclusively, any success they may have had in retarding inflation was very narrowly limited. In fact price control systems have usually crumbled when faced with the staggering problems that arise when they are needed most — that is, when inflation intensifies. Thus, as inflation gathered steam in the United States in 1966, and government standards for prices and wages were boldly and universally ignored, the prospects for intervening with any effectiveness, even selectively, grew hopeless. The "guideposts" of the President's Council of Economic Advisers gradually receded into the background and were soon all but forgotten, even by the public officials who had initially and so gallantly proclaimed them. Under the Nixon administration they were explicitly disavowed.

An Interim Assessment

Inflation, we have seen, springs mainly from an ailment that lies beyond the ministrations of the New Economics — namely, the imbalance in *structure* between the demand and supply of labor. Attempts to absorb the unskilled in the active labor force, simply by expanding demand, succeeds mainly in raising the wages and salaries of the skilled and highly trained, and along with that, the general price level. Periodic efforts to squelch inflation with the traditional tools of fiscal and monetary policy result mainly in creating unemployment. Sporadic efforts to control prices directly, by mandate, have been fruitless and short-lived. Cost-push and psychological factors persist as exacerbating elements in the relentless forward march of prices. It is as though the ship of state were off balance and government reacted by gently but persistently rocking the boat, a little more inflation and then a little more unemployment alternately spilling over the sides. The unavoidable conclusion is that the cure for instability — if cure there is — must lie beyond the New Economics, on which we have relied exclusively for so long. We shall pursue that path at a later point.

Meanwhile, we turn in the chapters just ahead to two

problems closely related to the national, and thus far futile, quest for stability. The first is poverty, which is obviously intensified by unemployment as well as rising prices. The second concerns the quality of life in a society beset by instability, extremely high taxes, the fetish of ever greater production, and the ubiquitous pressures of big business and big government.

※ *Chapter 5*

The Wasted Americans

AS VICTORY in Europe drew nearer in 1944, legend has it that President Roosevelt and Prime Minister Churchill once enjoyed a light moment together dreaming of postwar reconstruction. Churchill said he was prepared to underwrite the security of British subjects from the cradle to the grave. Roosevelt said he would provide security for Americans from birth to burial. Not to be outdone, Churchill said that he had been referring to the immediate postwar period only. Once recovery was achieved, his programs would care for Britons from womb to tomb. Roosevelt rejoined that his more mature programs would apply from conception to ascension. Such security, with all the public financial safeguards and collective services it suggests, no doubt epitomizes one popular version of the welfare state. Judged by the magnitude of public funds devoted to such purposes, the United States of Kennedy, Johnson, and Nixon has been no laggard.

In round numbers, about $100 billion annually was spent by government in the late 1960's for "social welfare" as defined by the Social Security Administration. The definition includes old age, unemployment, disability, and other types of social insurance, public aid to the needy, public health and medical programs, public housing, veterans' benefits, and public education. These expenditures came to $500 per year for every man, woman, and child in the United States, which is roughly equal to the entire national income per capita in countries such as Greece and Spain. When education is omitted from the list, the total of social welfare expenditures amounted to approximately $65 billion or about $325 for each person in the United States per year, which is still large enough to exceed the per capita national incomes in most of Latin America and Asia. Within the aggregate, about 60 percent went for old age, unemployment, and other social insurance, about 20 percent for relief payments and special services for the needy, and about 10 percent each for public health and for veterans' benefits.

Add the general affluence of the nation to this welfare colossus, and it becomes all the more difficult to believe that poverty, in any significant dimension, can remain a grim and stubborn reality. Yet, as the decade of the 1960's drew to a close, the number classified as "poor" by official government standards, even at the peak of the Vietnam war inflation, embraced more than one tenth of the total population. The abominable disease of racial discrimination, of course, plays a sinister role in this picture, but it is not the main cause of poverty. While all studies show that a disproportionately large number of Negroes are needy and jobless, the fact remains that 80 percent of the poor are white.

✌️ The State of Poverty

Although it provides small comfort for those in need, it
is worth recognizing that poverty is a relative concept.
Our notions of who is poor, and what level of living involves serious deprivation, differs sharply from time to
time and from place to place. Over time, the "poverty
line" keeps rising, as faithfully and about at the same pace
as does the degree of man's control over nature. If we
were to apply our poverty standard of today to the year
1929, after correction for price differences, we would come
to the astonishing conclusion that in that boom year as
many as 60 percent of all Americans were poor. Yet even
in the depth of the following depression no responsible
observer, including President Roosevelt, claimed that more
than one third of the nation was "ill-housed, ill-clothed,
and ill-nourished." Clearly our notion of what is necessary
as a "minimum" for "decent" family living has drifted upward noticeably since then.

Geographically, differences in the concept of poverty
are also great. Even the comfortable countries of Denmark
and Holland, both of which proudly hold that they have
eliminated poverty, would be embarrassed by the American standard, because judged by it, a substantial proportion of their populations are poor. All of which is not
meant to imply that our present American standard is ex-
travagant or wrong, but rather that it and all other standards of poverty are socially, not biologically, determined.

The official government yardstick used for distinguishing poverty in the United States is based on the cost of an "economy" budget that is supposed to provide "not much more than the minimum necessities," according to the Council of Economic Advisers. Naturally, the "necessities" are those conventionally judged as such by the dominant middle-class opinion of today. The budget itself was prepared by the Social Security Administration, and its cost is adjusted from year to year as prices change. In 1968 people were defined as in poverty if their annual money incomes fell below about $3500 for an urban family of four, $2500 for a farm family of the same size, $2200 for a nonfarm couple, and so on for families of different sizes in rural and nonrural areas. About 22 million individuals, comprising some 10 million households, were classified in the poverty category in 1968. They represented 11 percent of the total population.

Both relatively and absolutely, when judged by the government's standard, the poor were much fewer at the close of the 1960's than they had been just a few years before. In 1959 nearly 40 million individuals, representing 22 percent of the population, were classified as poor. Part of the improvement was due to the temporary influence of a war-inflated economy, which held unemployment down to levels well below the average of the past decade. But part was also due to the more enduring influences of basic economic growth and recent improvements in social security benefits and coverage. Whatever the causes, it is obvious that the increasing official concern over the poor in recent years was not occasioned by any expansion in their numbers, but rather by the growing frustrations and impatience of those who remained left behind in an era of extraordinary progress and prosperity.

Among the poor themselves there is possibly a greater disparity in income than there is in their social attitudes and way of life. At one end of the spectrum, especially among the Negro poor in the rural south, are those who actually — astonishingly in modern America — lack the physical means for survival. In a remarkable report of the Citizens' Board of Inquiry, the presence of hunger in these areas, of disease and early death from malnutrition, is documented by testimony and photograph. But such cases of extreme deprivation, although their number has not been accurately counted, are definitely a minority among those officially classified as poor.

From a census compilation taken in 1960, Herman P. Miller of the Census Bureau found that among families with incomes less than $3000 (a rough drawing of the poverty line in the prices of that year), 79 percent owned a television set, 73 percent owned a washing machine, 51 percent owned both a television set and a telephone, 65 percent had "adequate" housing including hot running water and a toilet and bath for their exclusive use, 19 percent owned a home freezer, and 14 percent had bought a car in the previous year. Even in Tunica County, Mississippi, the poorest county in the poorest state, where eight out of ten families are below the poverty line, 46 percent of all families owned their own automobiles. By most European standards, at least superficially, many of these families would be considered fairly well off.

It takes a closer look to judge them, and in particular an

understanding of the confused values that can couple in the same household a TV set and a mixmaster with a deficiency in diet and schooling. The objective picture, if not the cure, provided by Michael Harrington, Roger Lampman, Edgar May, the Council of Economic Advisers, and all others who have investigated poverty is much the same. The poor, far more often than not, are born poor. They lack the opportunities for education and health of the majority of Americans. They are mostly ignorant, unskilled, and insecure. They live in central city ghettos around the country and in rural backwaters largely but not exclusively in the south. Most of them work but are either hit frequently by unemployment, are so weakly motivated that they often quit, or can find only part-time or occasional jobs. Fatalistically, they see no point in planning. Their compulsive hunger for the material attributes of the more fortunate — the cars, clothes, household appliances — leads them into debt and cuts brutally into the resources they have for food, medicine, and housing. It was President Kennedy who said, in his 1962 public welfare message, that "the reasons for poverty are often more social than economic, more often subtle than simple." Perhaps the intensified frustration and violence of the poor (along with the national dismay it has caused) spring as much from these social as from economic factors — the growing awareness of their isolation and the gulf between their culture and that of the remainder of a fabulously growing society.

🎏 The Identity of the Poor

A question that haunts any observer of poverty is how so large a portion of the population can remain beyond the effective reach of a welfare system that seems, on the face of it, so lush and comprehensive. A look at the aged is instructive since for them, it might seem, the social security system had eliminated most if not all financial problems.

The Aged Poor. Over the past two decades old age benefits under the Social Security Act have been extended so that by the 1960's coverage was almost, though not quite, universal. The amounts of the benefits have also been raised periodically to help offset the inroads of inflation on their purchasing power. In 1968 somewhat more than 24 million beneficiaries under old age, survivors, and disability insurance received payments at an annual rate of $25 billion. Hardly anyone today questions the value of the program. While numerous experts wish to revise and improve the social security system, no responsible authority to this writer's knowledge proposes scrapping it. Perhaps just because of virtually universal approval, many have come to expect more of the system than it was designed to deliver. For the majority of aging couples who retire with at least some useful assets or income from other sources — a home with paid-up mortgage, a pension, or the help of sons and daughters — social security benefits are an adequate and important prop to their level of living.

On the other hand, for those who are forced to rely on social security *exclusively*, the benefits are in most instances insufficient. A glance at the schedule of payments shows why.

Benefits payable are scaled in large part according to the average income earned during some substantial part of the worker's life. At the lowest point on the scale, for a worker with average annual earnings of less than $900, the annual benefit payable for husband and wife would be $990. The widow, alone, would get $660. The family of a retired worker whose annual earnings were $3000, would get $2070; his widow would get $1380. Benefits rise in this way up to a maximum benefit of $3756 annually for a couple, or $2616 for a widow, payable to workers with average annual earnings of $7800 or more. However, most beneficiaries fall in the lower part of the scale. The reader should bear in mind that in 1950 (when most of today's retired were at the peak of their earning power), one half of all families in the United States had incomes of less than $3000. Even in 1960 more than one fourth of all families were in this class. Thus, the *actual* average benefit paid in 1968 to a retired worker and his wife was $1980. The average going to a widow was $1037. The poverty level income for a family of two in 1968 was $2240, and for a woman living alone, $1735. Clearly, for most of those *exclusively* dependent on social security, the benefits were inadequate — or at least less than that necessary for lifting them above the official poverty line.

The aged now receive some additional help from Medicare and other health facilities, and for the few uncovered by social security there are modest grants available from federal-state public assistance. Nevertheless, the overall picture is bleak. Of the 10 million poor households in the United States in 1968, 4 million were headed by persons aged 65 or over. Of all aged households, two out of five were classified as poor by the government.

Rare is the elderly employee who moves on at the end of his working days to the poet's "An elegant sufficiency, content — Retirement, rural quiet, friendship, books." Instead, most often he receives a double blow. He is dropped to a lower standard of living. His role as a useful member of society is closed. Psychologically as well as financially, many of the retired workers would be better off if they could continue to do some work — or were free, at least, to decide the issue for themselves. In this respect, the social security regulations are peculiarly perverse. For those under the age of 72, old age benefits are reduced by 50 cents for each dollar of earnings between $1680 and $2880, and by $1 for each $1 of earnings above $2880 — a 50 percent tax, in effect, on earnings in the first category and a 100 percent tax on earnings in the second. It is a strong deterrent, particularly when it is considered that employment always involves expenses (transportation and the like) that are not deductible from earnings. In the spring of 1969 the Nixon administration indicated its intention to modify these penalties on working, but not to eliminate them.

The situation of the aged helps to explain the persistence of poverty — specifically, about 40 percent of it. The other major group consists of men and women who move in and out of the labor force, seldom holding a full-time job for any extended period, and dependent for part or all of their incomes over the year on public relief.

🎏 *The Working Poor*

The widespread publicity won by the poor in recent years has no doubt alerted the public to many important aspects of their situation. One popular picture emerging from newspaper accounts, however, is a misleading carica-ture rather than a photograph. This depicts the poor, firmly convinced that work is the curse of the drinking classes, as greedily grasping for doles while eluding job offers with a deftness born of long experience. Typically, in the popu-lar version, the presiding head of the household is a woman who spends much of her time, at public expense, in mater-nity care. A statistical analysis compiled by the Social Se-curity Administration for the year 1966 shows a different picture.

More than half of all poor households, as the accom-panying table indicates, were *legally* headed by males, though for reasons given later this is almost certainly a gross understatement. More to the point, the tabulation shows that nearly all males under the age of 65 worked during the year. Almost half held full-time jobs through-out the year, though obviously at wages too low to lift them above the poverty line. Most of the rest were em-ployed intermittently or worked at part-time jobs. In addi-tion, one third of the female heads of households worked at full-time jobs and another one-third at part-time. Spo-

Table 1

The Work Experience of the Poor in 1966

(millions)

	Male head	Female head
Total Poor Households	5.6	5.4
Aged (65 years or over)	1.9	2.4
Under 65 years	3.7	3.0
Did not work	.7	1.4
Ill or disabled	.4	.3
Other reasons	.3	1.1
Worked at part-time jobs	.6	.6
Worked at full-time jobs	2.4	1.0
Employed all year (50 weeks or more)	1.5	.4
Employed part of the year	.9	.7

Detail will not necessarily add to totals because of rounding.

Source: The Annual Report of the Council of Economic Advisers, February, 1968.

radic unemployment obviously was a serious problem for most as it almost always is for the unskilled. Nevertheless, excluding the sick and disabled, the tabulation shows overall that nine tenths of the males and two thirds of the women did at least some work during the year. The data do not disclose how much more work the poor as a group may have done if they had been able to find and hold jobs *and* if they were not actively discouraged from doing so by public assistance regulations.

Perhaps no governmental program has been so widely condemned as public assistance, which is designed to provide financial aid to families with dependent children, the blind or otherwise disabled, and the aged uncovered by social insurance. The program functions as a branch of the Social Security Administration in a cooperative arrangement with the states. The writer knows of no general defense assembled in its behalf. As a sample of the more important critiques, we cite the general conclusion reached by the National Advisory Commission on Civil Disorders in its final report of March, 1968:

> The Commission believes that our present system of public assistance contributes materially to the tensions and social disorganization that have led to civil disorders. The failures of the system alienate the taxpayers who support it, the social workers who administer it, and the poor who depend on it. As Mitchell Ginsberg, head of New York City's Welfare Department, stated before the Commission, "The welfare system is designed to save money instead of people and tragically ends up doing neither."

It is to President Nixon's credit that he reacted constructively to such evaluations, with lengthy messages to Congress on public assistance and manpower training in the late summer of 1969. His plan for reform, along with others, is discussed in the following chapter. Yet prevailing practices are worth examining a bit further, both because they explain the persistence of poverty in the past, and because some of them, despite altered details and ruthlessly mangled acronyms, seem destined to survive even if and when the administration's new welfare program becomes law, as proposed, in 1971.

About 55 percent of public assistance is at present (1969) financed by the federal government on a partial matching basis with the states. Within very broad limits, however, the states are free to run the program as they wish, setting both the amounts of the grants and nearly all the eligibility requirements and other conditions. Naturally, these vary very widely. Except for a few states, notably New York, California, Wisconsin, New Jersey, Illinois, and Connecticut, the grants have been far below the poverty level. Toward the end of the 1960's the average payment under public assistance to families with dependent children, nationally, was about $145 per month per family, or about $36 per person. The range about the average was enormous, from a low of $9.30 per month per person in Mississippi to a high of $62.50 per person in New York.

The conditions of the grants, generally, seem mischievously calculated to militate against rehabilitation, self-help, or even stable marital relationships. Until recently, the penalty on earnings was as severe as possible. *All* amounts earned by welfare recipients were deducted fully from the public assistance they otherwise would have received. A 1967 amendment to the law modified this regulation modestly by permitting ambitious welfare recipients to keep the first $30 of their monthly earnings and one third of any earnings above that amount. For unskilled workers who have difficulty finding jobs, who are seldom sure how long they will last, who cannot earn much at best, and who have no guarantee that they can get on welfare again once they are off it, the penalty is more than mildly discouraging.

Some other unpopular practices of public assistance are now in the process of being modified, or in some instances, abandoned. The widely debated "man in the house" rule — the withholding of assistance from households containing an "employable" male — has recently been challenged in the courts. Surprise visits by social workers, to check on the incomes and assets of needy families, are being discarded in some states in favor of affidavits on financial status. The faults of such practices are obvious. For example, the National Advisory Commission concluded that one principal effect of the "man in the house" rule was to "break up homes and perpetuate reliance on welfare." On the other hand, despite modest improvements, welfare administrators still lacked a golden rule that would guard against abuses, with reasonable effectiveness, without levying a cost in unpleasant side effects.

Doles are a dismal aspect of any society, largely because they suggest hopelessness, sometimes slothfulness, and sometimes desperation. Were they associated, systematically, with programs for family rehabilitation, work training, job opportunities, general education, or child care, they might have an air of promise, improvement, accomplishment. They do not. It is perhaps because of this negative, discouraging element of the public assistance program that many of us are inclined to exaggerate its magnitude. The total amount paid out in direct aid to the needy at all levels of government averaged about $7 billion per year in the second half of the 1960's — a little less than the amount budgeted annually by the Defense Department for research and development. The funds reached only a fraction of the poor, and were kept so restricted by various limitations on eligibility — the *presence* of dependent children, the *absence* of an employable male, the absence of marketable assets, the required duration of residency, and so on.

What, then, of the vaunted $100 billion welfare program of the United States? Is it misdirected? Wasted? A little thought will recall that the welfare system is not in fact designed exclusively to help the needy. Social security benefits, veterans' benefits, workmen's compensation, and similar outlays go in larger part to people who are above the poverty line. Of all welfare expenditures, probably less than one-third provide aid, in money or in service, for people who are classified by the government as poor. Under these circumstances the persistence of poverty in the world's wealthiest country, despite substantial outlays on social welfare, should not be so surprising.

It is also no secret that some significant proportion of social welfare expenditures are wasteful. The Joint Economic Committee, in its annual report of 1968, likened the welfare system to "patchwork," lacking in discernible design or direction. Overlapping and lack of coordination has been disclosed by virtually every study group that has addressed itself to any important part of the social welfare system, ranging from the government's own National Manpower Policy Task Force to the U.S. Chamber of Commerce Task Force on Economic Growth and Opportunity.

Neither the whole nor any major part of the welfare structure escaped such criticisms, though the most telling blows were reserved for the programs in income maintenance, which we have described, and in vocational training. Thus, vocational training in 1969 remained uncoordinated either with public assistance programs on the one hand, or with the labor demands of industry and job placement on the other. According to a report of Sar A. Levitan, a consultant to the National Manpower Policy Task Force, present vocational programs "lack meaningful remedial education or training components" while the work experience provided "is of doubtful value." At the same time, numerous small and uncoordinated training programs have sprouted in recent years, and their costs mount up, no matter how ineffective they may be; $2 billion was budgeted for such projects in 1969. Misused public resources also help to explain the persistence of poverty.

How much poverty we have, where, and why, as we have seen, are not particularly easy questions to answer. They are childishly simple compared to the more penetrating question of what to do about it.

Chapter 6

Jobs or Doles

BY FAR the most common reaction to the welfare system of the United States today is dissatisfaction. Its complexity, its inadequacies, in general its high cost in relation to its low yield have won few friends and many enemies. Out of this dissatisfaction have developed two alternative ideas for radical reform. Both claim, in opposition to the present system, to be more comprehensive, more purposeful, and more efficient. The first of these alternatives envisages a system of guaranteed income allowances paid by government to the poor, or in some versions, to the entire population, with no strings attached. The second alternative centers about rehabilitation and jobs for all capable of work, while providing income support, where needed, for others. We shall consider each of these approaches in turn.

✌ *Guaranteed Income Allowances*

The chief advantage alleged for guaranteed income allowances is that they are simple, a merit as refreshingly rare in the world of welfare as diffidence on Madison

Avenue. They "cure" poverty by giving money directly to the poor. They do away with the "means test" and all the other paraphernalia of welfare work. In one form, originally advanced by Milton Friedman of the University of Chicago, the guaranteed income allowance would displace *all* other welfare measures — old age and unemployment insurance, public assistance, training programs, public health, and housing. In fact, Friedman — who is well known as one of America's most extreme and formidable apostles of private enterprise — has proposed ending public education too, provided income allowances are large enough for families to pay their children's tuition in privately run schools. But most advocates of guaranteed income allowances look upon them as a substitute, simply, for the present systems of "relief," known formally as public assistance and general assistance programs.

All the numerous plans devised to guarantee incomes have two characteristics in common: (1) they establish a minimum family income fixed at some tolerable or desirable standard, (2) they provide a subsidy up to this minimum to every family, either without conditions of any kind, or after "appropriate" deductions for the family's own earnings, if any. There are no plans of this kind operative anywhere in the world, although the very different "family allowance" systems of Europe and Canada are sometimes confused with them.

A central difficulty in guaranteed income plans, in the opinion of opponents, is that they suffer from an excess of their alleged virtues: they are *too* simple and *too* universal. They apply no means test as a condition for awarding allowances. They make no inquiries into a recipient's ability or willingness to work. Hence, they stand ready to provide guaranteed incomes not only to those who cannot work but also to many who can. They are likewise prepared to distribute some of their largess to families that do not need it, that is, to those well above the poverty line.

A natural question arises: will those capable of useful work have the same strong incentive to hold jobs if, without conditions or qualifications, they are guaranteed incomes when idle? A second and more important difficulty relates to the character of the poor as disclosed in the preceding chapter. Their return to the mainstream of American economic life and culture would seem to depend more on opportunities for education, vocational training, and jobs without discrimination, more on renewed hope and motivation, than on a simple guarantee of income. A case in point is the persistence of poverty and frustrated idleness in New York City, despite government gratuities that exceed the levels provided in most guaranteed income schemes. A pregnant danger of guaranteed income allowances is that they may maintain millions of families more or less permanently on the dole.

One aspect of the guaranteed income plan, not always apparent to laymen, has to do with a famous dilemma. It turns out, on the basis of simple arithmetic, that the income allowance systems must either penalize earnings severely, thereby actively impairing incentives to work, or they must tolerate a substantial amount of waste by paying subsidies to families far above the poverty line. The more they avoid one of these evils, the more they are forced to countenance the other. The dilemma can be illustrated by example, considering first two extremes and then the compromises that have recently been suggested.

A. *No Penalties, Maximum Waste.* This is the simplest plan of all. It proceeds by giving, let us say, $3000 annually (which we shall take, in the following examples, as a rough approximation of the poverty line) to every family in the United States, no questions asked. In particular, no penalty is imposed upon, or any other consideration given to, a family's earnings. The guaranteed income would go to the Rockefellers, the DuPonts, the Kennedys, and the hungry in democratic impartiality. For the 50 million families of the United States, the annual cost would be $150 billion, almost exactly the same as the entire federal government budget in 1967. But more important, less than one fifth of these funds would be going to the poor. From the standpoint of the tax bill, the four-fifths or more going to the others would represent the maximum possible waste.

The single merit of this plan, as compared to the other versions that follow, is that it does not *actively* discourage work, or at least not as much as *they do.* True, anyone who wished to do so, could abstain from work and live exclusively on his subsidy. Anyone with the inclination could take a year or two off, were he willing to rough it on the guaranteed income. Nevertheless, if he wished to improve his lot, and earn something on his own, he would not be penalized. In fact, even if he rose to the dizzy financial heights of an oil tycoon or a Hollywood star at his peak, his government subsidy would remain intact — a condition that would necessitate, for those who stayed on their jobs, taxes at least twice as high as they are today.

B. *Maximum Penalty, No Waste.* In this plan, allowances are made *only* to the poor. A family with zero earnings would get the full minimum income guarantee of $3000. A family with $1000 in earnings, however, would lose $1000 of its subsidy; it would receive $2000 from the government, just enough to bring it up to the poverty line. Similarly, a family that earned $2000 would sacrifice an equal amount of its subsidy; it would get just $1000 from the government. A family with earnings of $2900 would get a subsidy of $100. In this way the allowance would serve, exactly, to bring everyone who wasn't already there up to the poverty line, and no further. Families with earnings of $3000 or more would receive no subsidies, and hence, from the standpoint of the nation's tax bill, there would in this sense be no waste.

But notice the enormous price paid for this economy. Exactly $1 is deducted from the standard income subsidy for every $1 of a family's earnings, up to the full amount of the $3000 guarantee. This is tantamount to a tax on all earnings, up to $3000, at the perfectly confiscatory rate of 100 percent. In effect, under these circumstances, a man who took a low-paying job, say at $2500, would be working for nothing. True, he would receive a $500 subsidy. But he would have the same total income of $3000 (and would save traveling and other expenses) if he stayed at home. The incentive for work would be seriously reduced, if not eliminated entirely, even for those with greater earning power. For example, suppose that a family above the poverty line, with $4000 in earnings, was required to pay an income tax of 10 percent, leaving it with take-home pay of $3600. This family, of course, would receive no subsidy. But if the head of this household elected a career of TV-watching, or fishing, the family would receive its guaranteed subsidy of $3000, with no income tax to pay in most versions, and no working expenses in any case. How many breadwinners, in such circumstances, would stay on a job all year, full time, to bring in an extra $600, less expenses?

C. *Compromise Proposals.* The cost of the plan just described has been estimated at $12 billion. Much less expensive than the first, it is also much more unfriendly to industry. These two defects, extreme costliness (as in Plan A) and severe discouragement to work (as in Plan B), operate in a kind of pincer movement to vitiate the various schemes — known as "negative income tax" plans — that have been proposed as compromises. They all proceed by deducting *less* than $1 from the subsidy for each $1 of earnings, in the hope of encouraging work. The resulting allowances are incorporated, as a negative element, in the regular income tax schedule. Thus, if 50 cents were deducted from the allowance for each dollar earned, a family with $1800 in earnings would receive a subsidy of $3000 minus $900, or $2100. Its total income would be $3900. A family with $4400 in earnings would receive a subsidy of $800, figured by subtracting one half of $4400 from the $3000 standard allowance. Subsidies would go to all families up to the $6000 earnings level, at which point the deduction (one half of $6000) would fully exhaust the standard allowance. At incomes above $6000, the regular positive tax schedule would take over.

Since many families substantially above the poverty line would get allowances in this plan, it admittedly involves some waste and hence would be costlier than Plan B. More important, the extent to which it would sustain work incentives is uncertain. While being granted $3000 even when idle, the potential worker is assured that one half of any income he may earn on his own (up to $6000) will be taken away. If he took a job that paid $3000 annually, he would in effect be working all year to earn an extra $1500, less such expenses as bus fares, work clothes, and meals. His total cash income, including subsidy, would be $4500, but of course he would receive $3000 if he simply rested at home. Would he take the job? Would some, perhaps, decline regular jobs but work a bit on the side to conceal their earnings from authorities?

Of course, it is possible, arithmetically, to cut the deductions for earnings further — say to 25 cents for each $1 earned, instead of 50 cents, and this would provide some additional support for work incentives. Thus, a family that earned $2000 would lose only $500 of its subsidy, and its total income would be $2000 plus $2500, or $4500. Though simple arithmetically, the revision runs into economic trouble. A 25 percent deduction would mean that subsidies would go to all families with incomes up to $12,000, since not till this level was reached would the total deduction (one fourth of $12,000) exhaust the standard allowance of $3000. The remainder of the population, with incomes above that level, a fairly small minority, would be left to pay the total tax bill, which would obviously not be modest. Hence, as a practical necessity deductions cannot be made too small. It follows that the deterrent to work must remain fairly strong.

Nor is the dilemma solved by incorporating a sliding scale of deductions — starting with small deductions at low earnings levels, so as to encourage incentives, and gradually rising. The idea sounds much simpler than it really is. The change in tax or subsidy treatment of citizens from one income bracket to the next must be very gradual, otherwise there is the danger of having a family with, say, $5000 in earnings wind up with a smaller net income, after adjustment for subsidy or taxes, than a family with $4000 in earnings. Just as important, the fact remains that at *some* income level handouts must cease, and a positive income tax must take over. Neither sliding scales nor any other technique can avoid this hard reality. The higher on the income scale the cut-off point is, the more expensive the program will be, assuming the same standard allowance. The lower the cut-off point, the greater will be the damage to work incentives (because of the large penalties against earnings). Readers who are intrigued by the various mathematical possibilities of negative income tax plans, including sliding scales, are invited to examine the notes to this chapter provided on pages 183 to 187. There, some further examples are given, including a description of the schemes proposed by one of the more influential supporters of the negative income tax, the Brookings Institution. Although they provide a smaller standard allowance than

that used in our examples above, the annual cost of the
Brookings plans range up to as much as $49.3 billion.

Aside from its basic dilemma, between expense and incentives, negative income tax proposals suffer from certain
other difficulties. For example, it is no secret that small
businessmen, farmers, and some professionals have found
ways to hide part of their cash incomes from tax authorities, ingenious techniques that are simply not open to those
who live on wages and salaries. Yet, the negative income
tax eschews the means test and places complete reliance
on an "objective" arithmetic formula framed in terms of
the "objective" income tax schedule. It sweetens the pot,
in short, for the shrewd, more efficient or more unscrupu-
lous tax avoiders. A positive reward, in the form of a subsidy, is provided for those who can show little or no income, perhaps by deeding their property to others (legal),
by understating their receipts (illegal), or by other means.

A second problem has to do with the timing of payments for those who are eligible for subsidies. If the recipient had to wait for payment until his income deficit
had made him eligible, as evidenced in his tax return, he
would not receive aid when needed most. A plan allowing
citizens to anticipate deficits, through advance income
declarations, would run into all sorts of obvious difficulties.
For example, a subsidy paid in advance would have to be
returned, if actual earnings exceeded anticipations. Fluc-
tuating incomes among the wealthy are still another problem. A millionaire whose reported income in one unfortunate year fell to $1000 would be consoled with a govern-
ment check for $2500, under our 50 percent deduction

scheme. By a requirement for averaging incomes, or by similar complicated devices, this and perhaps some of the other subsidiary difficulties can no doubt be tempered or avoided. But not the basic dilemma, lying at the heart of the negative income tax. It is inherent, reminding us of Ring Lardner's hapless ballplayer, who "although he couldn't field, neither could he hit." Although the negative income tax does not preserve incentives to work, neither does it conserve the taxpayer's money. More poignantly, neither would it end poverty.

The latter truth is undoubtedly sensed by many of the poor themselves. A Gallup poll taken in January, 1969, showed that more than half of all persons earning $3000 a year or less either opposed or were doubtful about a guaranteed income plan.

D. *The Nixon Proposal.* The welfare reorganization, proposed by the Nixon administration to Congress in August, 1969, is essentially a guaranteed income plan. The guarantee applies, however, only to the parents of dependent children, and hence is not universal in coverage as are the others above. For such parents the guaranteed income would be $500 per year for each of the first two family members (say, mother and father or mother and child) plus $300 for each additional member. For the average family of four this would mean a guaranteed income of $1600. A family with a member who gets a job would be allowed to retain all of the first $60 of their monthly earned income, or $720 per year. On amounts above that, 50 cents would be deducted from the allowance for every additional dollar earned. Thus a family of four, with $2720 of earned income, would lose $1000 of its basic $1600 allowance, bringing its total income to $3320. A family that earned as much as $3920 would receive no benefit payment, since 50 percent on the excess above $720 (50 percent of $3200) would exactly offset the entire basic allowance.

In comparison with the guaranteed income plans described above, the Nixon approach is of course considerably more modest in the level of payments. It is also more circumscribed in that individuals and childless couples are not covered. (The aged and disabled, however, would remain under present assistance provisions, which in the Nixon plan would be slightly liberalized.) Aside from these, there is one additional, important difference. The income guarantee, Nixon's advisers realized, could damage work incentives as we have amply described above. Hence those who apply for benefits, in the Nixon plan, are required to register with a government employment service and to accept a suitable job, if offered; or to register in a training program if prevailing job opportunities and the aptitudes of the applicant make this feasible.

In comparison with the plan for guaranteed jobs and incomes we describe in the following section, the Nixon approach suffers from three serious flaws that are worth some elaboration—particularly since one of them is fundamental, common to all simple guaranteed income plans, and fatal to any real hope for curing poverty, or even substantially reducing it. First of all, the minimum income level guaranteed in the Nixon plan is low, too low even to cover basic necessities in metropolitan areas, although it might be sufficient for this in some low cost rural sections of the South. The plan we shall discuss would bring all citizens fully up to the poverty line, at a minimum, with appropriate differentials to reflect geographical variations in living costs. Second, the Nixon plan leaves part of the population uncovered, as already indicated. The coverage of our plan is universal. But these are details, serious enough, but easily corrected if Congress and/or the administration so determined. Not so for the third flaw, which is the failure of the Nixon plan to make adequate provisions for jobs. This last point is so crucial, so fundamental to the central economic problem of all welfare states, that is requires further elaboration.

Jobs are as essential to reform as wind to a sailboat, fuel to a motor. They are, after all, the ultimate channel through which the bulk of the poor can be absorbed into, and integrated with, the remainder of society. In the institutional setting of the stop-go economy, common to the United States and all other welfare states, the number of job opportunities inevitably remains less than that required to absorb the entire labor force, even after allowance for the minimum, frictional "between jobs" unemployment. The number of available jobs typically varies, growing larger or smaller, but at best very seldom, if ever, large enough for full employment. We have seen, in our discussion of the social menu curve, how the American economy has teetered back and forth between excessive unemployment and rampant inflation, never pulling wholly free of either one or the other. Thus, in full accord with the stop-go pattern, the Nixon administration tried desperately in 1969 to "dampen" the economy — that is, to exchange some of the excessive inflation of that year for some additional unemployment. And it did so even though the unemployment rate, at a bit under 4 percent, was a far cry from the true full employment 2 percent level. But dampening the economy, with the unemployment it spawns, obviously creates further poverty, which in turn adds to the rolls of those who must live on relief, or in the Nixon program on the $1600 (for a family of four) guaranteed income. The failure to provide jobs, of the Nixon and all other simple guaranteed income plans, is fatal to the avowed objective of fighting poverty. It would remain so even if the guaranteed income level of the Nixon plan were doubled, and even if training programs were proliferated on a gargantuan scale. Training without job opportunities is like a larder without food, as any engineer who lived through the Great Depression can testify.

The answer to the problem we have posed requires nothing less than a fundamentally reoriented approach to the problem of stability, so that full employment *without* inflation can be realized. Inevitably, as we shall see, there must be provision for public employment, as part of such a plan, as well as training and basic education for those who cannot get immediate jobs in private industry. But above all, the problem of instability must be frankly and boldly confronted. In the closing chapters of this book we try to do this, with presentation of a three-point program for achieving full employment without inflation. In the section below we describe one portion of that plan, that dealing directly with poverty.

Guaranteed Jobs and Incomes

We turn now to the other approach mentioned at the start of this chapter, and one that in the present writer's estimation holds much more promise. Curing poverty, it would seem, requires giving the poor what they most desperately need: this is not the handout of the negative income tax plan or similar income guarantees, but the opportunity to utilize their own capacities, in as full a measure as they wish, to earn their own livings on a par with other Americans. For some, this requires first of all basic education. For nearly all it entails practical vocational training or retraining, suited to their aptitudes as well as the needs of the market. For all, except the hopelessly disabled, it requires job opportunities, without discrimination with respect to race, sex, or age, so that acquired skills can be utilized. Given these conditions, government income support would be necessary or desirable only for those needy who are too old, sick, or handicapped to work at regular jobs, and as a partial supplement for those who, although capable of work, cannot earn a sufficient amount to keep them above the poverty line.

The requirements just outlined are obviously not met by the nation's present sprawling welfare activities, whatever their *nominal* objectives may be. Their disappointing lack of direction and ineffectiveness have already been amply described. The situation would seem to call for a fundamental redirection of national efforts, and I have therefore proposed establishment of a single federal agency to integrate all welfare activities into a fully coordinated, purposeful "Work-Welfare" program. In Chapters 8 and 9 we shall see that such an agency (which I call the National Service Administration, or NASAD) would be one element of a three-part plan to maintain overall stability, in an economy of full employment *without* inflation. For the moment, however, we are concerned with this agency's capacity to deal directly with the problems of the poor and to integrate the confusing jumble of bureaus, special programs, and other governmental units dealing with welfare, which are now scattered in the Labor Department, the Office of Economic Opportunity, the Department of Health, Education, and Welfare, and elsewhere.

NASAD, as I envisage it, would administer the Work-Welfare program through four closely knit branches or divisions:

A. *Old Age Assistance.* This branch would supervise an improved system of social security pensions and supplementary aids. It would eliminate the present penalties now imposed on the earnings of pensioners and would extend coverage to the few who still remain unprotected. On the assumption that enforced retirements may be more lethal than arteriosclerosis, anyone over the age of sixty-five could register, if he wished, in the Education-Training-Placement division described below. In other words, the elderly would be encouraged to remain active. However, those over sixty-five whose family income (including pensions and other sources, if any) were deficient, would be given supplementary old age assistance to bring them up to a minimum "guaranteed income" level.

B. *Education-Training-Placement.* This branch is the nerve center of NASAD. Except for the aged, all men and women who became eligible for unemployment insurance, or who wished to apply to government for financial assistance in any other form, would be required to register here. After interviews, written examinations, and other tests, applicants would be assigned to one of the following programs, all of which would be aimed at building or restoring their ability to help themselves: (a) education and/or vocational instruction, on a work-training basis, (b) placement service for jobs in private industry or government, (c) employment in NASAD's own work force, or (d) in the case of the sick or disabled, public health services. As will be explained in Chapter 8, the placement service as well as vocational training would be tied to a nationwide, computerized information system on present and prospective job opportunities. The vocational training would be organized, where feasible, in cooperation with private industry. All the services mentioned, including unemployment insurance and excluding, only, public health services, would be supervised in this division.

C. *National Service Units.* This branch would embrace the permanent work force of NASAD. It would consist of

(a) registrants with NASAD who possessed particular skills in demand in the national service units, (b) temporarily, some of those engaged in work-training programs, and (c) all qualified registrants who were not placed in other jobs after a reasonable period of education and training. The national service units would perform a variety of public services (described later, see pages 99–100) at state and local as well as federal government levels. In this era of rapidly expanding public needs, one may hope, no imaginative genius would be required to find worthwhile projects for the work units. One aspect of their activity, however, warrants emphasis at this point. Their functions would definitely include, insofar as possible, services useful for NASAD's own internal operations. For example, some work units would help to staff day nurseries maintained by NASAD for the assistance of working mothers. Some NASAD workers would be used to maintain the agency's buildings or other facilities. Some would perform clerical duties or even help in elementary educational tasks. But of course the great majority would be engaged in the wide range of public works, from anti-water-pollution projects and resource conservation to city beautification and the maintenance of recreational facilities, for which they are primarily intended. In these and in all the other national service unit functions, a contribution of immense importance is almost unavoidable — provided proper spirit and standards are maintained, and reasonably intelligent efforts are made to give employees a legitimate pride in their work.

D. *Public Assistance.* All registrants with NASAD whose family incomes remained below a fixed minimum would receive public assistance allowances in amounts sufficient to bring them up to that minimum. The fixed standard would be equivalent to that now established by the Social Security Administration for the measurement of poverty, with differentials for size of family and location. For an urban family of four in 1969 it would amount to about $3500. The recipients of public assistance would include (a) those needy who were unqualified for training or work because of physical or other handicaps and (b) those whose earnings were insufficient to bring their total family incomes up to the poverty level margin, including the part-time workers in NASAD's education and training programs.

Thus, no less than the negative income tax plans, the Work-Welfare program would guarantee a minimum income, but unlike them, it would not provide *automatic* allowances. The emphasis, instead, is on rehabilitation and job opportunities. Permanent subsidies would go only to the aged and to those who were certified, because of some deficiency, as unable to work. But support for training, or jobs, would be available for all others. Since nearly all the beneficiaries would be productive, the net cost to society would be much less than that of the plans featuring wholesale handouts. Since education and training are at the core, the program would be curative, tending to diminish steadily the number of those who are today economically and culturally estranged from the remainder of the country. The deprived, and the poor in general, would be gradually absorbed into the self-supporting, self-respecting community at large.

🕊️ *A Note on Family Allowances*

Liberal Americans often suffer from a misplaced inferiority complex when confronted with the words "family allowance." Somehow, the phrase seems to imply income maintenance programs, common to the European countries and Canada, that are overwhelmingly superior to any and all of the welfare measures now prevailing in the United States. Defective as the latter are, the impression is mistaken on all counts. The family allowance systems have not functioned primarily to maintain incomes and do not provide substantial grants in any case. As Martin Schnitzer mildly comments, in a study prepared for the Joint Economic Committee in 1968, "The person who thinks that the European countries are doing things better than we are in the whole area of social assistance may be in for a disappointment."

In general, family allowances are paid to all families, regardless of their incomes, that have more than one child. For example, in Great Britain an allowance of $1.80 per week is paid to a family for its second child, and an additional weekly allowance of $2.04 for each child after the second. For an average family of four this would yield an income of less than $100 per year. For a family of five the allowance would come to only $199.68 annually. In France, which possesses the most generous of all family allowance systems, the income provided for a family of four is $182 per year. Of course, it is true that most European countries offer other forms of public assistance and also provide a variety of public services. But no one of these measures, nor all of them together, succeed in guaranteeing a minimum income for all in any one of these countries.

As already suggested, family allowance systems were generally not intended for that purpose. For example, in France the objective was explicitly to increase the birth rate. In Canada and Great Britain the aim was to stimulate purchasing power and boost the level of employment at the end of World War II. It is ironic that the payments provided in all existing programs are so small that they leave virtually no impression on poverty, wherever it may exist. Yet, since payments are made to all families with children, regardless of income, they are expensive. A plan proposed by Daniel P. Moynihan (at present writing, adviser to President Nixon), which is somewhat less generous than that of France, would cost American taxpayers $9 billion per year — almost as much as the service charge on the entire $360 billion national debt.

In a recent stay in Europe, this writer had occasion to discuss problems of welfare assistance with officials and economists nearly everywhere on the Continent and in Great Britain. Not one wished to recommend family allowances to the United States. Many said that they would like to find some way of terminating the system in their own countries, taking account of the small payments made to the poor, the pointless extravagance of allowing grants even to the wealthy, and the possibly perverse effect on population, even if mainly psychological, in an era in which ever more of the globe suffers from too many people.

❧ Chapter 7

Quantity and Quality
in Economic Life

DESPITE THE UNPARALLELED wealth of
the United States, Americans are seldom encouraged to
rest on their laurels. Deliberately savoring the fruits of
our industry, relaxing as a way of life, and not merely on
vacation, would suggest slothfulness, as un-American as it
is depressing to sales and profits. Instead, we are solemnly
warned by nearly all authorities that new obstacles lie
ahead and that we must grow economically to meet them.
The spurs are applied by both government and business
to impel the nation forward to ever higher pinnacles of
productivity. Some $17 billion annually is spent on ad-
vertising to lure Americans into wanting and buying a
constantly expanding cascade of goods and services. In
government, at all levels, politicians point to a perpetually
rising backlog of unfilled public needs, so that it seems a
moral crime to resist a tax increase, unspeakable to suggest the possibility of a reduction. The time for letting up,
for self-congratulation, we are universally advised, is not
even on the horizon.

Indeed, given the many-sided pressures, it is probably
true that Americans work harder than the people of any

other developed country. As Teyve exclaims, in *Fiddler on the Roof*, it's "Tradition!" Compared with Europe, rivalry among American business executives, scientists, academicians, and other professionals is more widespread and personal, and hours of work are longer and more intensive. Competition is more spirited among American business firms. Shopkeepers work longer hours. Officially, the work week is shorter for American factory labor, but overtime is more frequent than in most other countries, discipline is greater, and holidays fewer. Furthermore, 4 million Americans in 1968 worked nearly around the clock as *dual* job holders. No doubt this intense application to work, along with bigger and better capital equipment, helps to explain America's superior productivity. Whether it makes a commensurate contribution to the quality of life may be more debatable. Perhaps the tensions of the American scene help to explain why, despite their greater wealth, the life span of males in the United States is three or four years shorter than in most of the other developed countries.

Automation and Growth

Any industrial country, with a sophisticated stock of capital and an educated citizenry, is virtually certain to progress economically, though the pace and the nature of progress may vary. Scientific knowledge expands and with it, the degree of man's control over nature. The economic yield, technological progress, has characterized all of modern history. Its latest phase, automation, is distinctive in its use of automatic control systems and electronic computers, but its ultimate impact is the same as that of earlier advances: an increase, year by year, in the amount the nation can produce per man-hour of labor. Continued technological advances in the United States, plus the better educational level and skills of the labor force, promise to increase output per man-hour over the economy as a whole by about 3 percent per year in the decade ahead. Cumulated over a single generation (twenty-five years), that rate of advance would amount to a potential increase in production of about 100 percent per man!

That potentiality is a glowing promise, and we shall soon discuss how it may be utilized or thwarted. But before we do, note that what seems like a promise to some, often appears like a specter to others. Witness the words of George Meany, president of the AFL-CIO: "Automation can be a blessing or it can be a curse . . . There is no longer any question in my mind as to the direction in which automation is going today. There is no element of blessing in it. It is rapidly becoming a real curse to this society." The sentiment behind Meany's words is reminiscent of the machine-destroying riots of the late eighteenth and nineteenth centuries, and like those riots, they contain a mixture of justification and futility. Opposed to his position is the evident fact that technological innovations have provided the major substance of mankind's laborious advance from ignorance and want; around the world people work to live, not live to work, and all the help they can get is welcome. But in support of Meany's consternation is the concrete impact of technological advance on particular individuals: those whose skills and productive capabilities are rendered obsolete. Thousands of families in coal towns from Bluefield to Harrisburg have been on relief for years because of the introduction of the giant automated Push-Button Miner. Hunger in Mississippi, and the crowding of northern ghettos, are in part a by-product of the mechanical cotton picker. The displacement of men by machines in these and in other industries (especially basic steel, petroleum refining, tobacco manufacturing, textile mill products, lumbering, and railroad transportation) has been widespread and ruthless. Though few would want to set the clocks back, a legitimate question may be raised about the timing and the manner of such changeovers.

Even under the best of circumstances, technological unemployment is a serious side effect of progress, but it is a side effect for which there can and should be effective antidotes. Most important is the availability of an organization such as the National Service Administration described in Chapters 6 and 8, to which displaced workers can be promptly assigned for placement in other jobs, aid, advice, retraining, and assistance in moving when required. Necessary also is a mechanism for maintaining a truly stable and prosperous economy, for then the task of shifting workers from one industry to another becomes more easily manageable. These are essentials, but in themselves they are not sufficient. The fact is that, humane considerations aside, technological innovations are typically adopted too rapidly and too suddenly from a coldly *economic* point of view. The reason is that the businessman naturally bases his decision purely on an accounting of the relevant *business* costs; neglected are the *social* costs of the changeover, which must be borne by the economy at large.

Thus, for a businessman the wages of a fired worker are counted fully as a saving. When the total savings of this kind exceed the costs of introducing and using a new automated method of production, it becomes mandatory, by profit maximizing rules, to make the changeover. But from a national point of view, the full wages of workers are *not* saved when they are fired. There are costs of maintenance and renovation involved, even though the private business concern is under no legal obligation to meet them. There is inevitably a delay (at present, sometimes extending to years) before the displaced worker can find other employment. Meanwhile, society maintains the worker and his family even though he contributes nothing, currently, to production. Notice that this is true whether the worker lives temporarily on his personal savings, unemployment insurance, or ultimately on relief; the fact remains in any case that he is a consumer, but not a producer, and hence appears only on the *cost* side of the nation's aggregate ledger. The worker may require retraining, which also bears a cost. He may have to move, incurring other expenses. All these are measurable costs which must be weighed in the national balance, if not in the individual firm's accounts, before deciding whether it pays, for the nation, to introduce a new method of production. There are also, of course, intangible costs — the blow to the displaced worker's pride, the adjustment, at least temporarily, to a lower income, the uprooting of the family if it becomes necessary to move.

From a national point of view, it does not pay to introduce a new method of production until its incremental yield to society is great enough, at least, to meet all the costs involved. Were we to act on this principle, changeovers would be more gradually and carefully paced, allowing more time for workers to be placed in other jobs, or for some to retire, than is customary now. Ideally, the timing of laborsaving innovations should be worked out in cooperation with appropriate government authorities (in the plan presented in this book, with the labor market specialists of the National Service Administration), who would take full account of aggregate yields and aggregate costs. More crudely, some of the social costs of changeovers could be imposed on the responsible business concerns, so that it would affect their decisions, by requiring ample notice to workers before firing along with a schedule of generous severance payments. It should be emphasized that a more deliberate pacing of innovations would help expand the national output, rather than retard it. It would accomplish this by imposing on private business a responsibility for exercising the same concern for the efficient use of human beings (which of course they do not own), as they now voluntarily demonstrate in their use of machines (which of course they do own).

≥⊩ *Productivity and the Future*

Technological advances, along with education, are certain to present a potentiality for much greater output in the years ahead, however they are paced. As mentioned above, the prospect is that output per man can be doubled within twenty-five years. Within just ten years, output per worker could be 35 percent higher. If such prospects seem to give rosy promise of a new era, we can gain a sobering perspective by looking back at our past. We had similar opportunities ten years ago. Superficially, the potentialities then present were realized, at least in that output per worker grew at nearly 3 percent per annum, close to the same rate that seems likely for the years ahead. It brought more goods and services, some diminution of poverty, but certainly not a new era. Indeed, the general way of life today seems much as it was then, with just as many unsatisfied wants, at least as much tension, and just as much energy expended in the endless pursuit of higher incomes, additional attributes of affluence, and the expanding obligations that go with them.

It is equally sobering to examine the recent report of a responsible research organization, the National Planning Association, on our future economic prospects. The prospects of productivity, as viewed by the NPA, are the same as that given here — a projected increase of about 3 percent per worker annually. At this rate the gross national product could be expected to rise to $1120 billion by 1975, compared with $850 billion in 1968, assuming prices are unchanged. Average personal income per family, as projected by the NPA, would rise to $11,600. The *beginnings*, at least, of a new era? With some of our major social problems put to rest? With a noticeable lift in the cultural and aesthetic values of life? Perhaps a more relaxed business and social environment? Not perceptibly, as the NPA figures it. Projecting our future "needs" and "wants" on the basis of past and present trends, the NPA found that the gross national product, at $1120 billion in 1975, would fall some $170 billion short of our national aspirations. The need would be for much more, not less, of the material things, even after the giant step forward, raising the vision of old John Q. who holds two jobs to pay for the swimming pool he never has time to use.

🌿 Growth and Time

When urged constantly to produce more, an intelligent citizenry has an obligation to inquire, at least, about directions. Many of our most important needs will not necessarily be satisfied by producing more, indiscriminately. The hunger that exists in Mississippi, Alabama, and some other parts of the south sits side by side with "overproduction" on our farms. Annual model changeovers in the automobile industry — at an average addition to cost of $700 per car — lead to faster obsolescence and more auto production, but not directly to better transportation. Tax increases, unless tied to specific, testable objectives, may be dissipated in the service of special interests or in waste. Economic growth, meaning more goods and services, is desirable only when it leads to desirable ends.

Citizens who feel overpowered by the blandishments of advertisers, and humbled by the lofty goals of governmental bodies, can benefit by recalling a simple truth, often forgotten: *all economic choices may be reduced to decisions concerning time.* The proposition is obvious when applied to a shipwrecked sailor — the classical case — alone on a deserted island. Whether he wants more fish, better fishhooks, a larger shelter, or more leisure are questions that he must resolve through the allocation of his time among all its possible alternative uses. While less obvious, the truth holds in the same way, and just as inexorably, for the people of a nation. The labor force, including all who contribute to the country's output, represents a certain number of man-years, approximately 80 million in the United States. It may be used in a variety of ways, and more or less fully. If work days were lengthened, rest periods cut, and time used as intensively as possible, physical output could be expanded very substantially. If pressures were relaxed, and more value placed on leisure and recreation, the labor force would produce much less — less, that is, in terms of the measurable goods and services that are sold on the market. Whether we undertake more manned flights in space, more cancer research, or more international combat, or build larger and faster cars in greater abundance, better schools, or clear the ghettos — all are questions, fundamentally, of how we allocate the labor force's time. Advertising and taxes, equally, are demands on a people's time.

American visitors abroad are inevitably impressed by a significant international difference in the disposition of the average man-year between industry and leisure. It may be a result, essentially, of the more vigorous and uninhibited advertising industry in the United States, the "business culture" dominant in our society, or less obvious but nonetheless deeply imbedded habit patterns. Americans seem to have a hunger for goods, and a relative disregard for their leisure time, unmatched by most other people in developed countries. This eagerness for material things, and the readiness to put out for them, as already suggested, explains in some measure the greater productivity and abundance in the United States; this connection, in turn, leads some Americans to speak disparagingly of the indolence and inefficiency they believe they encounter elsewhere. But some observers perceive behind this difference in behavior a significant difference in values. For example, Professor Harry G. Johnson, who divides his teaching equally between the London School of Economics and the University of Chicago, has noted that "whereas Americans are happy to tell you about the efficient gadgetry or the high cost of their housing, Britons bask in the age or the cheapness of theirs; and whereas Americans will tell you in detail why they bought one brand of household equipment rather than another, Britons will explain precisely why they chose one continental country rather than another to spend their vacation in." The British (and other Northern Europeans), according to Johnson, take pride in the practice of "make do and mend." Americans are more responsive to "Get with it and spend."

Neither Harry Johnson nor the present writer would suggest that Americans, therefore, ought to ape the European way of life, or that Europeans would necessarily be better off if they copied Americans. The lesson of the preceding argument is simpler but more important. It is that *more* is not necessarily *better*. Economic growth is not a good in itself. We may purchase more or less of it, within limits, but our currency is that most precious of commodities, time. It is not a decision to be made lightly. In fact, whether we should have more economic growth, or less, or any at all, can be judged intelligently not in the abstract, but only concretely, in terms of specific objectives and their alternatives. It is not inconceivable, in some instances, that we may achieve a positive good (say, better preventive medicine) by giving up an expensive nuisance (say, supersonic transport airplanes). When urged to move the country forward, citizens have an obligation to inquire, where? Toward what destination?

🎌 Growth and Decisions

The questions are not easily answered. Society has a momentum that seems to carry individuals along, independently of their deliberate decisions, to destinations selected, as it were, by higher authorities. United States output, per capita, has grown so fast that it is now twice as great as that of the richest countries of Europe. If the end of economic activity is human happiness — if we do indeed work to live instead of living to work — one would expect to see a reflection of this tremendous material progress in the American way of life. Of course we do. Americans have, for instance, more cars, TV sets, electric toothbrushes, dishwashers, refrigerators, pleasure boats, and consume more gasoline, cosmetics, tobacco, steel, paper, and beef per capita than any other people.

But such evidence is still on the material side. Of greater interest are the more fundamental facets of human well-being. Have the enormous strides in production been matched in the *quality* of American living — in the range of interests and activities, the amity of social relations, the gentleness of people, the relaxed enjoyment of leisure, the relaxed enjoyment of work, in the concern shown by citizens for others, the cultural level, health, tolerance of new ideas, family contentment? It would be a tall order to try to measure whatever such gains there might be. But in 1968 the average family income in the United States, after adjustment for price increases, was nearly double what it had been just twenty years before. Did the quality of life show comparable improvement?

It would go too far to say that Americans operate an economic treadmill, working for a better life but making little discernible progress. Closer to the truth would be the proposition that much of their time and energy is dissipated in productive activities, often environmentally imposed, that contribute less than an appropriate share to their welfare. Some important opportunities for a better life, for an enhanced quality of life, are therefore missed.

And if this is true, it must be that somehow our labor and resources, in some considerable part, are misdirected; somehow our national decisions on what to produce and how much are at fault.

𝕒 Household Decisions

A half century ago the brilliant American economist Wesley C. Mitchell wrote an essay entitled, "The Backward Art of Spending Money." His thesis was that the variety and complexity of consumer goods, and the diversity of brands and makes, had far outdistanced the average household's ability to make sensible choices. The concrete facts available about most goods — their durability, limitations, distinctions from competitors — were few, and about some, they were entirely absent. Nor would anyone have the time, patience, and expertise to gather all the relevant facts, assuming that they were accessible, for any large proportion of the goods he buys. In the decades since Mitchell's article, with the flowering of the welfare state and the further proliferation of new and complicated goods, the problems of consumers have multiplied.

Ignorance, however, is just one of the problems. The demands of consumers, far more than in Mitchell's day, are subject to the powerful influence of advertisers. To be sure, households must know what is for sale, when, where, and at what price. But the bulk of the Madison Avenue dollar does not go for providing such essential information. With a skill that puts some other arts to shame, advertising has succeeded in directing household demands — in steadily extending the horizons of consumer wants and the willingness of Americans to labor energetically to satisfy them. Is it economically wasteful to stimulate demand with planned obsolescence, fabricated status symbols, reiterated subliminal motivations, false promises of irresistible charm or eternal youth? Some may argue that it is every citizen's right to rank ostentation, or even frivolous nonsense above cold, functional utility, if he so wishes. But even granting that right, the inescapable fact is that advertising succeeds with remarkable effectiveness in *distorting* consumer demands. The virtues of marketable goods — all irresistibly glamorous or miraculously efficient — are magnified beyond limit. Obviously, the items not for sale, whether leisure time in general, museums, tennis, bird-watching, adult education, or a game of catch go unmentioned. As John Kenneth Galbraith has pointed out, the whole range of government services goes unmentioned, except in occasional derogation. Advertising inculcates the compulsion to spend, for which the citizen may mortgage his future as well as the present; it is not, and cannot be, concerned with the consumer's allocation of time, the development of his interests, the variety of his enjoyments — except those purchased from the sponsors.

Aid to Consumers. The defenses available to consumers against ignorance and undue sales pressure, while perhaps not impregnable, could be quite potent if it became politically possible to use them. First of all, constructive efforts can be made to improve the knowledge of consumers about what they are asked to buy in the marketplace. The nation's households are in this respect the neglected sector. Business is generally able to specify and test the goods it buys with its own resources. Agriculture receives constant guidance on its purchases from government, free of charge. Consumers, of course, have their advertising, but the net contribution to knowledge from this source may well be negative. At best, the "free" advice advertising provides would be worth the price — if it were really free. What is needed is a medium through which household goods can be objectively tested and compared for their efficiency, range of functions, maintenance costs, comforts, safety, convenience, and so on, and through which the results of these analyses can be made widely available to the public. More generally, consumers need a vigorous authority to represent their broader interests, to protect them against the output or other activities of industry, and sometimes of government too, that impair their health, degrade the environment in which they live, and jeopardize their safety.

The answer would seem to be a consumer representative in the federal government with cabinet rank, who would consolidate, strengthen, and extend existing bureaus, such as the Food and Drug Administration and parts of the Federal Trade Commission, that now have some concern for consumer affairs. One of the new activities that this cabinet officer could organize would be the advisory service for consumer goods suggested above. It is true, of course, that several private organizations now sell information of this kind, but they are small, little known, relatively expensive, and lack official status. An expansion of such services, so that virtually all families are reached, would rather clearly require public support. One method, among other possibilities, would be for the government to subsidize a number of private consumer testing and advisory services, each specialized in some given category of household goods. The services would be sold to the public at a nominal fee. The difference between the cost and price (including allowance for a public utility type profit) would be met by the subsidy. The government's Department of Consumer Affairs would provide whatever general supervision of these activities might be required to insure objectivity and scientific standards.

A second course of aid to consumers — the traditional and classic source — is business competition. In its absence, and unless protected by other means, consumers can be systematically deceived and otherwise exploited. But as Adam Smith observed nearly 200 years ago, competition is a fragile flower requiring careful cultivation. The current possibilities for improved cultivation, while not novel, are important. A further reduction in tariffs and other barriers to foreign trade, preferably in line with those of our trading partners, would encourage international competition. (A *mutual* reduction, incidentally, would probably improve rather than impair the U.S. balance of payments.) A more vigorous enforcement of the antitrust laws might forestall the collusive agreements and the wave of mergers and acquisitions that in recent years have strengthened monopoly. Competition is not a completely untarnished benefit to society; it is occasionally wasteful and sometimes destructive, particularly of natural resources. Yet with proper safeguards it is an essential element of an efficient and progressive economy. Of more immediate importance at the moment is that competition helps to extend the choices available to consumers, to improve the quality of goods, and to lower prices.

Finally, it may be time for society to protect itself, directly, against advertising. If advertising does distort consumer decisions, and if above a certain level, it does qualify as a public nuisance, then some reasonable limitations may be justified. Perhaps the best tool is the tax "disincentive." In this plan a certain minimum amount of advertising would be allowed tax free, the minima to be established for the firms of each industry on the basis of past experience. *Excessive* advertising, that is, expenditures above the minima, would be subject to a tax. The rate of taxation would rise progressively as a firm's advertising outlays rose further above its established minimum.

Whether an advertising tax is politically feasible, given Madison Avenue's pervasive influence and talents for persuasion, is an intriguing question. It is tempting, but probably wrong, to conclude that the outlook is flatly hopeless. Americans once sang an old song that says, "The best things in life are free"; given a modern hearing, the idea could spread, though no doubt with the sober emendation, "*Some* of the best things in life are free."

❧ Public Decision-Making

Not so long ago, as historians reckon time, the role of government in the United States was relatively modest and, especially at the federal level, commonly considered innocuous. Only in times of burning national issues such as slavery, turn of the century trust-busting, election periods, or war did the eyes of the populace focus on Washington. Even then, the scope of activity was often minuscule by present standards. President Theodore Roosevelt's army of trustbusters consisted of five attorneys and four stenographers. In any case, except in emergencies, the federal government was typically ignored; only special interests, when sufficiently motivated, gave it appropriate attention. Unless spotlighted by major scandals, as they sometimes were, state and local governments received much the same treatment.

That the situation has changed is an understatement; it has been revolutionized. It is in the nature of the welfare state that government play a critical role, directly or indirectly, in nearly every branch of economic life. Government at all levels now absorbs nearly 30 percent of the nation's total output. It takes about the same proportion of the national income in taxes. How this money is spent, and how government uses the resources at its disposal, is obviously a critical element in the welfare of the American people.

Money and Efficiency. Perhaps the chief obstacle to efficiency in government lies in a modern tendency to glorify the *size* of public activities rather than their quality or content. The tendency has several sources. One of its older roots stems from the prestige of government administrators, which, like that of military officers, varies directly with the number of employees they command and the magnitude of the appropriations at their disposal. Thus, a public official normally advances in salary and renown by growing in stature with the size of his own agency, or of course by moving to another one with a greater growth potential. In any case, the system provides no automatic, or even any very likely, reward for reducing costs. The common business practice of attempting to produce any given good or service at the *least* possible cost is a doctrine that has many formal advocates, but few devoted practitioners, in the public service. The failing is well known, and there have been some notable efforts to overcome it. Secretary Robert McNamara's "whiz kids" violated some hallowed traditions in the Defense Department in the early 1960's with their attempt to introduce systematic cost-reducing techniques. President Johnson pushed the same techniques, under the imposing title of the Planning-Programming-Budgeting System (PPBS), with a directive issued to all departments of government in August, 1965. The move has spread also to some state and local governments. Thus, the fad of incorporating "programming" divisions in various bureaus of government, at all levels, has definitely caught fire. There is no evidence, however, that they have yet had a significant effect on government practices, except for an expansion in the public employment of mathematicians. Nevertheless, when, and if, they do, their beneficial impact will be primarily on the costs of providing given government services. The more difficult and fundamental question of determining which government services to produce, and how much, which projects to expand, contract, terminate, or start, lies almost entirely beyond their province.

Paradoxically, one of the most important obstacles to the making of rational and efficient decisions in the public sector stems from the fact that for so long in the United States the public sector was relatively neglected. The prolonged and flagrant disregard of essential public needs, described so well in the works of Professor Galbraith, produced a powerful reaction — a swing of the pendulum that for some of the more enthusiastic supporters of big government yielded to a curious *reductio ad absurdum*: the proposition that each additional dollar of public spending, regardless of purpose, *necessarily* provides an addition to the public welfare. The view makes sense not in sober judgment, but only as part of a desperate effort to right what was considered a grievous wrong. It is expressed by Galbraith (in *The Affluent Society*) with an extraordinary exhortation to liberals: "The rational liberal, in the future, will resist tax reduction, even that which ostensibly favors the poor," if lower taxes mean reduced public spending. The same view appears in the recently proposed "tax-sharing" plan, which is based on the "fear" of its authors (principally, Walter W. Heller, of the University of Minnesota, and Joseph A. Pechman, of Brookings Institution) that the end of the Vietnam war would bring a substantial drop in federal taxes. It proposes instead that some major part of the postwar "surplus" in federal funds be turned over to the states with no strings attached, that is, to use for whatever purposes they wish.

All such efforts to promote public spending per se, however well intended, share the same weakness: they retreat from the obligation to discriminate. Wasteful public projects, those that merely benefit special interests, those that are simply obsolete, and those that satisfy the most urgent public interests, are all on the same footing in this framework; they are equally encouraged. Examples in each of these categories are not difficult to find in current government budgets. Thus, about $3 billion is spent annually for agricultural price supports, although nearly all economists agree that the program was justified only as an emergency measure in the Great Depression. The stockpiling of "strategic" nonferrous metals goes on at public expense, although most authorities believe that its need ended with World War II. New urban freeways are constructed, blotting out entire neighborhoods and jamming city streets, although the majority of experts not connected with the automobile industry favor subways. Space research mounts into the multibillion-dollar category, although its major beneficiaries are the particular business corporations, military personnel, and scientists that serve it.

One could go on, though no doubt everyone's list of questionable projects would not be identical. But the examples cited are not as important as the fundamental principle they illustrate. If the growth of government is to promote, rather than drain, the public welfare, the electorate must be enabled to make intelligent choices. It must be enabled to stop as well as to start projects, to contract as well as to expand them, after judging their relative benefits and their costs.

Benefits and Costs. The goods and services provided by government, unlike business, are not normally sold on the market. Therefore, their values are not, and cannot be, automatically measured in dollars by the interaction of demand and supply. In most cases their benefits are so diffused in the population, and so intangible even though important, that they cannot be measured in dollars even by indirection, that is, by comparing them with similar or substitutable goods purchasable in the marketplace. The preservation of natural resources, the cleansing of air and rivers, education, the administration of justice, medical research, aid to the blind and the aged are examples. For some purposes we can measure such services by their cost, but that procedure avoids the very point at issue: *how can the benefits of a public project be compared with its cost, so that, in effect, the public can choose those that offer the most for the money, and reject others?*

There is no precise answer even in theory, nor should one be expected. Benefits must be judged qualitatively; an informed electorate, ideally, would express its judgment through the political process. But an informed judgment requires the relevant facts on benefits and costs. This in turn imposes a burden of self-evaluation on government itself which it has in nearly all instances avoided, for it requires stating as fully and clearly as possible just what the current benefits of each project are, along with the expenses. Where possible, the benefits should be described in quantitative terms, such as the number of students enrolled at various levels of school or the number of people who have used a publicly maintained recreational area. But numbers are seldom sufficient to evaluate a service, and it is not always possible to use them in any case. What is essential is that a clear, factual, and verifiable statement be made of the benefits, quantitative and/or qualitative, that may be realized from each public service, and that the full cost of each service also be included.

Such statements would then lend themselves to the rating of projects, by the administration, by the opposition, by citizens' committees, and by the public in general. The opportunity would be presented for substituting meaningful public debate for the persiflage and empty rhetoric that too often obscures public issues. Those projects rated by majority judgment as top priority items, with imposing benefits in relation to costs, would be natural candidates for expansion. By the same token, those at the bottom of the list would be candidates for contraction or extinction. The system would not maximize the net benefits of society with mathematical precision — as if that were possible — but it would at least move government service in the right direction. Certainly, obsolete programs, clearly wasteful projects, or those catering to special interests would have a more difficult time surviving under the glare of informative, factual, nationally publicized analysis.

Present budgetary practice, it is interesting to note,

contrasts sharply with this scheme. The tendency now, at all levels of government, is to give full publicity to *new* public needs, the rich rewards they will yield, and the urgency with which higher taxes are required to finance them. The emphasis is on lofty sentiments and additional spending. Existing programs are barely mentioned except to provide them, usually, with the annual increments necessary to "keep them in line" with the growth of the nation. As related by a group of scholars in a 1967 report to the Joint Economic Committee of Congress:

> Budgets are almost never actively reviewed as a whole in the sense of considering at once the value of all existing programs as compared to all possible alternatives. Instead, this year's budget is based on last year's budget, with special attention given to a narrow range of increases or decreases.

The scholars would not have been amiss to have mentioned that increases regularly outweigh decreases, and usually by large amounts. Nevertheless, it is not so much that the present budgetary process automatically guarantees a steady growth in government: new programs are constantly born; old ones rarely expire. It is that the growth is uncritical, undiscriminating, and proceeds more or less independently of the public will.

🙟 *Toward Quality*

Bigness in business and government is a dominant component of modern economic life and is likely to remain so. Indeed, despite romantic exhortations to the contrary, the size and power of business and government seem certain to continue to grow along with the nation's technological skills, its capacity to produce, its population, and the economic interdependence that ties the destiny of all members of the population inextricably together. The prospect is a promise as well as a threat. Big business is the seat of America's well-known productivity. Big government is essential for ordering and managing a society that becomes ever more complex and interrelated. The challenge to modern democracies everywhere in the world today is to shape their development so that the economic system remains responsive to the public's desires and makes the maximum possible contribution to its welfare. The answer is definitely *not* a blunt, quixotic assault on the *size* of business and government, not a fruitless effort to turn the wheels of history backward. This approach serves only to deflect attention from the real issues: the need, in the public sector, for enhancing the power of individual citizens to make conscious, discriminating decisions on what government shall do and the need in the private sector for strengthening the influence of individual decisions on what and how much to buy and produce — in counteraction to self-serving advertising, public relations, and other calculated propaganda.

Paradoxically, the individual in modern society stands in danger of being run by the institutions he ostensibly created to serve him. This state of affairs is symbolized by the prevailing tendency to glorify gross quantity over quality, in the reflexive response that takes ever more

money and ever more output as the necessary and sufficient answer to national and international needs. More
money, and never mind just how it is spent. More output, and never mind whether the products last, are really
useful, pollute the air, encourage highway accidents, de-
face the countryside, contaminate the streams, destroy
wildlife, or stimulate cancer in humans. It is a trend that
runs counter to the conservation of *time* — that is, of
human life — and counter to rational judgment and discrimination that are the essence of quality, however much
it may serve the reigning hierarchy of corporation executives and public officials. We have considered several
proposals aimed at redressing this basic distortion, at forti-
fying the individual's role in shaping the economy's decisions; but these or any other amelioratives are of subordinate importance. The real hope lies in a reawakening
of the public, in its rising educational level, which promises a better grasp of economic and political issues, and in
its will to use fully the democratic procedures that are at
its disposal.

Chapter 8

A Plan for Stability:
Part I

THE ECONOMY of the welfare state sails in a leaky sloop, careening uncertainly between a Charybdis and a Scylla. If it were feasible to disregard inflation, no one can sensibly doubt that unemployment could be quickly reduced to the barest minimum possible, just as it was in two war periods. Vigorous fiscal and monetary measures could expand the nation's total spending relentlessly until, as the Employment Act of 1946 has it, jobs were available "for all those able, willing, and seeking to work," or in other words, until unemployment had been reduced to the ultimate minimum of 2 percent that we have defined as full employment. It is true that the sharp inflation at this extreme right end of the "social menu" curve (see the diagram on page 34) would cruelly punish one important segment of society — the pensioners, schoolteachers, and all those many others whose incomes are relatively fixed or "sticky," that the swift price advance would place a premium on speculation and divert resources from legitimate productive activity, and that in international markets this briskly cantering inflation would soon become insupportable as our exports dropped, our imports rose, and the gold and other reserves for meeting the imbalance quickly diminished. All this must be granted. And hence full employment, with abundant inflation, cannot and has not been tolerated for very long by any nation that has the power to avoid it.

Equally untenable is the extreme at the other end of the social menu curve. Inflation too can be conquered, within the bounds of existing institutions, but only if it were feasible to ignore unemployment. Aggregate demand could be dampened to a point sufficiently low so that the upward trend of prices would grind finally to a halt. At least 7 percent of the United States labor force — or some 5.5 million workers — would then be unemployed, judged by past experience. The national output would be reduced and its normal year-to-year expansion, required to accommodate a growing population and for other reasons, would be emphatically retarded. Higher taxes would be needed to meet the heavier burdens placed on public assistance agencies and perhaps on the funds available for unemployment insurance. Joblessness always strikes first and hardest at the most vulnerable groups — the disadvantaged Negroes, the unskilled, the illiterate, the school dropouts, the chronically irresponsible, and the aging. The miserable sinkholes of poverty in which they dwell would deepen.

Present institutions provide no solution to the problem posed by these alternatives, except the compromise of evils that navigates an uncertain course usually between the two extremes, but sometimes touching one or the other. In this chapter and the next one we shall present a three-point program that attempts much more than this.

The objective is to salvage the best of the two extreme positions so that full employment — *true* full employment — can be maintained without inflation. Perhaps surprisingly, since this goal has so easily and consistently eluded the welfare states up to now, the proposed plan calls for no radical institutional departures. It does call for a significant revision in the techniques of fiscal policy, a brisk and thoroughgoing coordination of presently available programs on manpower, poverty, welfare, and public employment, and a massive extension in the use of one of them. It is in the master plan that embraces and guides them all, more than in the substance of any one of the measures, that the true novelty lies. Nor does the program require huge additional appropriations that would penalize one sector of society, through exorbitant taxes, for the presumed benefit of another. The intent, instead, is to create an environment in which each individual will be enabled, and helped where necessary, to utilize his productive capacities to the limit of his ability and desire. The "objective function," as technical economists like to say, is the economic welfare of all.

☙ Point One: Public Employment,
Training, and Placement

As we saw in Chapter 6, there are at present almost innumerable agencies that impinge in one way or another on the life of the unemployed worker and on those who are otherwise idle and in need. They receive income from unemployment insurance, from several types of public assistance, and of course from private charities. A variety of agencies located in the Office of Economic Opportunity and in the Departments of Labor, of Commerce, and of Health, Education, and Welfare provide training and retraining programs, adult education, maternal care, family guidance, area development, urban development, housing assistance, information on job opportunities, employment bureaus, publicly financed jobs, and other services. In each of these areas, in turn, special projects abound, among them New Careers, Work Incentives Program, On-the-Job Training, MDTA Short-Term Training, Economic Development Assistance, Job Corps, Opportunities Industrialization Centers, Community Action Manpower, Special Impact Program, Model Cities, the Cooperative Area Manpower Planning System, Urban Renewal, Volunteers in Service to America, Community Work Experience, Vocational Rehabilitation, Head Start, Upward Bound, and so on.

Nor do these various projects, programs, and agencies supplement one another in any neat pattern aimed at systematic rehabilitation — say, to remove the idle from the dole, provide them with skills that are truly in demand, and get them into jobs where they can use them. Instead, the several students who have examined the maze of institutions that focus on unemployment and poverty have been struck most forcefully by pointless duplication and glaring lack of coordination. In any event, the paucity of results is indisputable. The stop-go economy operates about as usual with serious pockets of poverty persevering side by side with an ever-faithful inflation. In the twelve years from the beginning of 1957 through the end of 1968 unemployment averaged more than 5 percent of the labor force while the consumer price index rose by 25 percent. True full employment, as we have seen, implies an unemployment rate of no more than 2 percent. The integrity of the dollar as a medium of exchange requires that the consumer price index, on balance, be stable.

In this first segment of the three-point program for stability presented here, it is proposed that all activities bearing on unemployment, welfare, and poverty be fully coordinated, housed in a single agency, and aimed systematically, as they can be, toward achieving full employment without inflation. For ready reference, I have called this coordinating agency the National Service Administration or NASAD, and we have already seen in Chapter 6 how its services may be used in an attack on poverty.

We come now to this agency's central function as a stabilizer. Briefly, NASAD's chief contribution would be to alter the nation's demand for labor, unskilled versus skilled, so that full employment *without* inflation may become a real and practical possibility. It would provide immediate jobs for the unskilled, without inflating the nation's overall spending, and would at the same time improve the long-run supply of skilled workers through coordinated work-training and placement services. In other words, NASAD would insure full employment while simultaneously *making it possible for the nation to avoid inflation.* The achievement of price stability is then reinforced by the two remaining components of the three-point sta-

bilization plan presented here, which are described in the
next chapter.

NASAD and Full Employment. For an understanding of
NASAD's stabilization role we need to recall an earlier
analysis (page 56) of the composition of the labor force.
In summary, the labor force of the United States may be
thought of as consisting of two quite distinctive segments.
First, there are the professionals, the technicians, the well
educated, the talented, the skilled, and the experienced —
those, in short, whose services are nearly always in solid
demand. This group is well adapted to the modern technology and the world of commerce, and its members, practically all of them, are employed continuously, as data presented earlier showed. Second, there are the unskilled,
inadequately educated, untrained, and inexperienced, who
are in general unadapted to a technological era that requires a higher level of literacy, vocational preparation,
and mental and physical discipline than ever before. This
latter group, a small but important minority in the total
labor force, stands at the very end of the nation's long
employment queue, crowding the alcoholics, the chronically debilitated, and the depraved who are all but unem-
ployable. They work on occasion but not many have
steady jobs that keep them busy year after year. Since
their productivity is low, business often finds that their
contributions to revenue are not sufficient to cover their
wages, even when these are fixed at the minimum allow-
able under law. When aggregate demand is sufficiently

high so that it does pay industry to hire most of the unskilled and untrained, one can be certain that in nearly
all of the nation's other markets for men and for goods,
demand is greater than supply and inflation is rampant.

In other words, those who are typically jobless can be
kept at work, but only at the cost of stiff inflation. Then
it pays industry to hire the unskilled to haul, lift, run
messages, sweep, carry, fetch coffee — anything to conserve the time of the trained and the skilled whose services are so expensive and so scarce. In the long run, an important part of the solution is to improve the skills of the
unskilled, wherever that is possible, so that their productivity will be high enough to win them jobs at noninflationary
levels of aggregate demand. The National Service Administration would help to do this, but it would also do more.

Within two weeks after applying for unemployment
insurance benefits, a jobless worker would register with
NASAD. If his qualifications, and the demands of the
market were favorable, he would be enrolled with the
agency's nationwide employment service and placed in a
job in private industry or government. Otherwise, after
suitable tests, he would be enrolled in one of the several
branches of a work-training program run or organized by
NASAD. In either case, with minimum delay, he would
be restored to his role as a productive member of society.
Moreover, the relatively few jobless who are uncovered
by unemployment insurance, together with the able-
bodied who remain on public assistance, would also be
recruited for similar work-training programs or job placement.

Any tour around the country, taken by an inquisitive reporter, would disclose the remarkably narrow purviews within which many people live. Many workers stranded in some of the decaying towns of Maine are utterly unaware of the living conditions and skill requirements in the towns or cities of Michigan, Idaho, or even Connecticut and Rhode Island. The unemployed of Appalachia and the ghettos of New York and Chicago often have no notion of where they could go, or even what training they could acquire in their wildest dreams, in order to better their lot. The employment services of the National Service Administration would be designed to fill this gap in information, as well as to remove the blocks of inertia, helplessness, and indolence that sometimes supplement it. Employment bureaus established at strategic points around the country would systematically obtain information about job openings; they would cooperate with, and coordinate, the activities of specialized private employment agencies in this task. The information acquired would be computerized and centralized in NASAD, would help to shape its training programs, and would be used directly for the placement of workers. A system of grants plus loans would be established to meet moving expenses and thus improve the mobility of workers.

Bringing jobs and men together would itself reduce the rate of unemployment and by improving the mobility of manpower would help dampen inflationary pressures too. But *prompt* placement through this system would be possible only for those who already possessed the skills and aptitudes required by the market — a group that would be a distinct minority among the commonly unemployed.

For the majority, the work-training program would be required. Undoubtedly, the bulk of the recruits to the employment rolls of the National Service Administration would fall into one or the other of the following two categories: (1) the unskilled and semiskilled and (2) workers whose skills, because of technological change, had become obsolescent. All such workers would be employed initially by NASAD at the legal minimum wage and would be assigned to one of three possible work-training programs: (1) subsidized on-the-job training in private industry, (2) subsidized on-the-job training in state and local government, and (3) a work-training-basic education project run by NASAD itself. Assigned to jobs for at least part of their time, they would become active producers at once; from one fourth to one half of the work day, however, would be allocated to acquiring the basic education and the new skills necessary to fit them for better roles, both as citizens and as workers. The particular assignment and training provided would depend on the aptitudes of the workers, on the requirements of the market as reported by the NASAD employment bureaus, and on the requirements of NASAD itself. As recruits became qualified, the nationwide placement service would take over. "Graduates" would move on to permanent jobs in private industry, local, state, or federal government, or, generally as a last resort, the "national service units" of NASAD.

Notice that as the potential productivity of NASAD registrants was raised through training and education, the employment of many of them at prevailing wages in pri-

vate industry would become feasible, and with no necessary pressure on the price level. In fact, their addition to
the supply of competent workers would tend to dampen
wages and prices. But doubtless, such a happy eventuality
would not be possible for all NASAD recruits, even in time.
There would be those who, simply because of their own
limitations, could not acquire the more demanding skills.
One of the challenging tasks of NASAD would be to provide useful activities for this basically low productivity
manpower, to fill some of the gaps in their education, and
through on-the-job training help improve their ability to
perform meaningful assignments, however rudimentary
these might be.

This lower productivity group together with the tran-
sients — those who after a time go on to other jobs —
would comprise most of the permanent, publicly employed
staff of the National Service Administration. In a nation
that has been notoriously neglectful of public services, it
would not be difficult to find things for them to do. NASAD
workers could be recruited for useful service at any level
or branch of government, state and local as well as federal,
to assist in a variety of capacities in the construction or
maintenance of recreational facilities, vocational training
centers, rest homes, children's camps, day nurseries, li-
braries, and cultural centers, or in slum clearance, resource
conservation, city beautification, medical assistance, rat
extermination, and sanitation, among an almost endless
number of social needs that have been only partially satisfied if at all.

The range and importance of useful services that can

be performed by the unskilled in the private as well as public sectors should not be underestimated. Pride and earning power can be built into even the simplest jobs — as janitors, messengers, cleaning women, handymen, garbage collectors, park attendants — if incentive and instruction is provided for performing them efficiently. For example, about 1.5 million mothers with nearly 5 million children are now on public assistance. Many of them, no doubt, feel that the money they could earn, say in domestic service, would be too little to justify the effort — not to mention the difficulties of leaving their children. But suppose NASAD provided day nurseries (staffed by NASAD mothers) for the care of their children, and also training so that they could occupy better-paying jobs. Even in domestic service, a woman capable of cleaning three apartments faster and better than she could previously do one will earn more and also think more of her occupation. Learning the tricks to any trade can be a source of satisfaction as well as added income.

NASAD and Stable Prices. Obviously, the National Service Administration would achieve full employment, since all the idle would be systematically prepared for and placed in jobs in industry, government civil service, or in NASAD. In fact, the efficiency with which manpower was used would be greater than would appear from the usual statistical indicators. The many idle, but potentially productive men and women on public assistance are not normally counted as part of the "labor force," and hence are not included among the unemployed, but they would also be put to work. So would many involuntarily "retired" workers — unskilled as well as upper grade professionals — some of whom live on poverty level pensions. The important question remains: how would the operations of NASAD help to combat inflation?

Our earlier analysis showed that under present circumstances the only way to relieve excessive unemployment is to expand aggregate demand to inflationary levels. As the nation's spending increases by sufficiently large amounts, and as prices and wages rise to suitably lofty levels, job openings can be created even for most of the unskilled; only under those conditions does it pay business to hire them. And the inflation can be deliberately intensified, as it has on occasion among the welfare states, creating more and more jobs straight to the point of full employment. The National Service Administration provides a route for reaching this point without inflation. In effect, NASAD would radically change the shape of the "social menu" curve so that the nation would enjoy an option that does not now exist: full employment *and* stable prices. It would accomplish this in three ways:

1. At present there is no systematic and efficient way of bringing men and jobs together; the process is merely left to chance, which is haphazard and slow. Pockets of unemployment frequently prevail only a few miles from vacant jobs requiring the same skills that the idle possess. Bear in mind that we are referring to job openings that might exist even if the nation's unemployment rate were

as great as 7 percent and prices were perfectly stable. Many jobs at such times remain unfilled for long periods because of labor immobility, ignorance, and indolence. If a way were found to bring such jobs and men together more expeditiously — with greater speed and certainty — average unemployment could be reduced at least by some significant amount without the need for raising the nation's total spending to inflationary heights. NASAD's employment service would do this through the use of its comprehensive information on job openings and job applicants, its system of nationally coordinated employment bureaus, and the financial and other assistance it would provide to encourage labor mobility.

2. Inflation stems partly from the scarcity of many types of skilled personnel. Through its various training and education programs, as well as by improving labor mobility, NASAD would increase the supply of scarce personnel and thus dampen the tendency for inflationary increases in many wages and salaries. Notice that by this procedure it would be placing formerly idle men into jobs that were already there — that is, it would be reducing unemployment, and again, most significantly, without the need for a prior increase in the nation's aggregate demand.

3. The residue of the unemployed, those who were not placed in jobs through the processes just described, would be employed by NASAD in its National Service Units. Since the aim is to avoid inflation, as well as raise employ-

ment, it is essential to understand that this would *not* be accomplished through deficit spending. Indeed, the expenses of hiring the unemployed and all other costs of NASAD (*less certain offsetting savings*) would be balanced by an appropriate increase in taxes. In this way the overall expenditures of the nation — aggregate demand — would be maintained at a noninflationary level, a matter to which we return in the following chapter. The worried taxpayer may note that the tax rise would be moderate, for part of NASAD's funds would come from substantial savings — among them the cost of the numerous, uncoordinated "antipoverty" programs presently in operation, which NASAD would replace, plus a significant reduction in unemployment benefits, public assistance, and other relief which would no longer be needed in such large amounts. As shown later, the net cost would be small by any standard.

The contrast with prevailing techniques is worth some further emphasis. Under present conditions full employment is achieved, if at all, only by boosting the nation's aggregate demand to inflationary heights. In the plan proposed here, full employment is realized, essentially, by altering the *structure* of the nation's aggregate demand. NASAD stands ready to hire the unskilled, who would otherwise find jobs only in inflation. The shape of the social menu curve is thereby dramatically altered, so that full employment *and* stable prices become a practical possibility. Realization of this possibility, in practice, depends also on two remaining elements of the stabilization program, to which we turn in the next chapter.

✻ *NASAD Functions in Outline*

Before rounding out our stabilization program, it may be useful to recapitulate the functions of the National Service Administration:

1. It would maintain a continuous inventory of the nation's job opportunities and of the nation's idle, all of whom would be registered with its comprehensive nationwide employment service. Specialized, privately operated employment offices would be incorporated, for purposes of national planning, within the government system. Employers would be *required* to report job openings with NASAD, and when possible, to give advance notification of vacancies as well as layoffs. Jobs would be offered to registrants in line with their qualifications, though, naturally, employers would remain free to hire within or outside NASAD rolls. Where needed to bring jobs and men together, NASAD would provide grants and loans to finance moving and new housing.

2. Men and women not promptly placed in jobs through the employment service would be assigned to one of the following three programs, depending upon their aptitudes:

a. On-the-job training in industry. NASAD would subsidize placement by paying one-half the going wage for these workers during a limited training period.
b. On-the-job training in state and local government

service. Here, too, NASAD would pay one-half the payroll costs during the training period.

c. On-the-job training and education with NASAD. Many of these workers would be trained for permanent national service employment. Others would be sent to private educational institutions for instruction in subprofessional, skilled, or certain types of "unskilled" occupations. Particular assignments in these categories would depend on actual and prospective needs in government and business as well as the aptitudes of candidates. All registrants with NASAD who needed it would be given basic education in reading, writing, arithmetic, and citizenship through facilities arranged in cooperation with the public schools. The activities of the Employment Service and the various training programs would be coordinated at all times, so that swift placement could be accomplished as instruction was completed. People would not be prepared (as they often are in the small, highly fragmentized, and uncoordinated programs of today) for jobs that do not exist. It has even been said of one of the present programs that a man had to learn a trade in it, in order to discover what kind of job he was out of.

3. NASAD would maintain a permanent staff of public employees, partly to help administer or expedite the functions described above, but mostly to man a variety of National Service Units. These work units would be distributed around the country, in accord with needs, would operate in cooperation with all levels and branches of

government, and would provide the numerous public goods and services, some of which were mentioned earlier, that are now partly or entirely neglected despite their usefulness.

We come now to the remaining two segments of the stabilization program.

Chapter 9

A Plan for Stability:
Part II

ECONOMIC STABILITY, in the present proposal, would rest on a three-legged stool. The first support, the National Service Administration already described, is concerned mainly with full employment. The second support, consisting of a new technique for flexible fiscal controls, is aimed directly at avoiding inflation. The third support provides a vehicle for improving the relations between capital and labor, so that full employment and stable prices can be sustained in an environment of lively economic growth. Like the three legs of a stool, the three supports function cooperatively, and the entire structure would topple or at least wobble with the failure of any one.

✠ Point Two: The Theory of
Refundable Taxes

Let us start with a situation not very different from that in which John F. Kennedy took office in 1961. We shall simplify only slightly. The unemployment rate is steep — 7 percent of the labor force. Prices, however, are perfectly stable. The immediate problem is to correct the first condition (unemployment) without sacrificing the second (stable prices). The solution is provided, tentatively, by the first point of the program for stabilization presented here, as already described. The National Service Administration would as promptly as possible absorb the unemployed in its training, placement, and public employment programs. To achieve full employment, as we have defined it, the required number to be absorbed (at least until training and placement yielded results) would represent 5 percent of the labor force, leaving the bare minimum of 2 percent unemployment. To be sure, those receiving NASAD funds would soon be spending all or most of their new incomes, thus tending to swell the GNP and also to stimulate an upsurge in prices. But the first point of the plan also calls for a rise in taxes, sufficiently high so that the reduced spending of taxpayers just offsets the additional spending of NASAD's new beneficiaries. Hence prices would remain as they were — that is, stable. At the same time unemployment would be cut to its minimum, providing a combination of economic goals that had never before appeared together in modern history. Let us suppose that the gross national product prevailing in this situation of full employment without inflation is $900 billion.

There are two problems that arise from this first approach — this initial solution — both of which would require attention. One which we shall deal with later relates to the large number — 5 percent of the labor force (about 4 million persons) — that would have to be accommodated by NASAD, at least at the beginning, either in placement services, training, or actual employment. While not intolerably large, it would be clearly burdensome and expensive. The other problem that concerns us now is this: given the favorable start just described, what would keep the GNP at the noninflationary, full employment level of $900 billion in the period ahead? The movement of business is like that of the open sea, with changing tides and currents, turbulent storms of activity alternating with stagnating episodes of calm. Even though the government's own tax and spending policies were neutral, a surge of private business investment could boost the GNP well above $900 billion, stimulating inflation; a drop in business investment could depress the GNP far below $900 billion, creating more unemployment and stalling economic growth. A technique is obviously required for regulating the national income so that it will remain at a level that will place a minimum burden on NASAD without provoking an inflation. In our example that would mean a GNP of $900 billion. If kept at this level for the time being, and permitted to expand only gradually in line with the economy's long-run growth, the nation would enjoy full employment without inflation.

The problem posed, that of regulating the overall volume of the national income, is a familiar one. It is, in fact, the very aspect of stability on which the New Economics placed exclusive emphasis, and for which its magic formula was developed: when inflation threatens, raise taxes or lower public expenditures; when depression threatens, do the opposite. There are several reasons why, in practice, this formula lost its magic, all of which are given in Chapter 3. One of these relates to the cumbersomeness, the inflexibility, of the two tools of fiscal policy upon which reliance was placed. As explained in Chapter 3, it is neither possible nor desirable to change tax rates or the volume of public expenditures with the frequency and the speed required to offset the trends of inflation and recession that recur constantly and most often, unpredictably, in private business. In the use of these tools, as we have seen, there were inherent and irremediable lags, so that at times tax changes and fiscal maneuvers in general were more unsettling to the economy than they were stabilizing. A new tool of fiscal policy is required that can operate with sufficient flexibility and speed to counter the instability of business effectively. This is the role of the second element of the three-point plan for stability proposed here.

A Flexible Fiscal Policy. If a surcharge on the income tax liability of a household or a corporation were imposed, with the agreement that the amount of the surcharge would be *refunded* on a specified date, the charge levied would in effect be a *compulsory loan* made by the household or the corporation to the government. Its status as a loan would be even clearer if the surcharge were repaid with interest. The proposal of Point Two is that a system of such compulsory loans and repayments be used for expanding or contracting the nation's aggregate demand as required. The scheme would work in the following way.

When inflation threatens, and it is necessary to choke off purchasing power, the President would order a flat per-

centage surcharge to be added to the liability of each taxpayer. Thus, if a family's normal tax liability was $1000,
and if the surcharge were fixed at 10 percent, the full
liability after the surcharge would be $1100. However,
the stabilization increment of $100 would be in the form
of a compulsory loan rather than a tax. It would bear
interest, figured cumulatively at the rate currently prevailing in savings banks or saving and loan associations.
More important, it would be definitely refundable. Each
loan would be repaid, at the latest, at the end of three
years, or earlier if so ordered by the President.

In order to permit the system to operate effectively in
both directions — that is, in expanding as well as contracting the economy when desired — Congress would
establish a *stabilization trust fund*. Within limits set by
Congress, the President would have authority to order
compulsory loans, which would be paid into the fund, or
repayments of loans, to be paid out of the fund. Repayments would be decreed by the President whenever the
economy was slack and expansion was required. Each individual loan, however, would at the outside be redeemed
at the end of three years.

If in the long run it appeared that repeated loans were
necessary, and payments into the fund greatly exceeded
current payouts, it would signify a fundamental lack of
balance — an enduring inflationary bias — that could
properly be corrected by an increase in taxes. Once taxes
were raised in this way, full employment and stable prices
would prevail without the *repeated* need for compulsory
loans. In the same way, if it were found that maintaining

stability required repeated payouts, or repayments of loans, so that the stabilization fund declined steadily, a persistent imbalance in the other direction would be signified. It would suggest an enduring *deflationary* bias that could properly be corrected by a tax cut. But these would be deliberate, carefully planned adjustments in tax rates that would occur rarely. The swift, push-button changes needed for stabilization would be effected through compulsory loans and repayments.

It is essential to recognize the important advantages this plan has over the traditional tool of tax changes. In the first place, it would enable government to take action swiftly, bypassing the interminable debates, political maneuvers, and other delays that have always featured proposed changes in taxes. The President would have authority to order loans or repayments at his discretion, which means whenever and as soon as his technical advisers convince him they are necessary. Congress could appropriately accord the President such power since it would not involve relinquishing its traditional control over the nation's purse strings. The surcharges, as already explained, would be loans, not taxes, and just as important, they would be duly "sterilized" in a stabilization fund so that they could not be used for financing public expenditures. Compulsory loans would be paid into the trust fund and then held there. Outlays from the fund would be made only for the repayment of loans.

Secondly, although loans would reduce immediate purchasing power, and repayments would expand it, unlike taxes they would not alter the fundamental financial positions of businesses or households. Loans would be tantamount to forced savings — assets which would grow with interest (perhaps 5 percent cumulative), and which would surely become liquid within three years or sooner. Thus a business investment that had been undertaken on the promise of a 10 percent yield would still hold the same promise in the long run, whether a compulsory loan had been added to the regular corporation income tax or not. In contrast, a substantial tax boost of the usual kind could transform a once profitable venture into a failure.

Yet, by contracting or expanding the income immediately available for spending, compulsory loans and repayments would affect the current outlays of households and business much as tax changes would. The difference is that they would not alter the *permanent* incomes of either consumers or business. Therefore, the longer term financial plans of both, so important for personal security as well as stable economic growth, would be unaffected. For this reason the President could feel relatively free to order loans or repayments swiftly, when required, without fear of the self-defeating repercussions that tax changes often have on the planning of business and consumers.

Finally, as a permanent fixture, the compulsory loan plan would remove tax increases or reductions, and public spending as well, from the emotionally charged arena in which hastily considered decisions are demanded to meet the immediate emergencies of excessive unemployment or inflation. A more rational approach to taxation and spending may then be possible. For example, the elimination of wasteful items in the federal budget could be debated on its merits, relieved of the irrelevant requirements of economic stabilization. In the same way, the case for closing tax loopholes could be urged on the proper grounds of equity, efficiency, and morality.

The last point is of key importance just because it has been so widely neglected in recent years. Wasteful public outlays have been lightly excused, especially in slack times, on the grounds that they create employment. Sudden and sometimes incentive-crushing advances in tax rates have been justified as necessary to defeat inflation. Yet, in a more thoughtful mood, practically all economists and political scientists would agree that public spending should be confined to legitimate public needs, and that the question of their magnitude should be settled on how we value these public services as compared with the private resources and private goods that we have to give up to get them. Our tax rates, at the same time, should be established in relation to the necessity for financing these public services, at levels consistent with the long-term growth capacity of the nation at full employment. Such fundamental objectives become distorted or obscured when confused with the immediate and transitory requirements of stabilization, as they were so notably during the prolonged tax debate of 1967 and 1968. The compulsory loan, or refundable tax plan makes a more rational and responsible federal budgetary program possible.

An Illustration. In the example with which we started, if business investment rose and the gross national product began to move above the ideal $900 billion level, the

President would order a surcharge increment to be added to the current tax bill. This compulsory loan could be reflected in the current withholding payments of individuals and corporations within a month, in contrast with the several years now normally required to get a tax change enacted and effective. As the available purchasing power of the nation was reduced in this way, its spending would necessarily diminish. The inflationary movement of the GNP would be checked and stability restored. The new compulsory loan payments, meanwhile, would swell the Stabilization Fund.

In the same way, if business activity lagged, current tax surcharges would be reduced (or, if necessary, redemption of outstanding compulsory loans would be accelerated), and the net disposable incomes of individuals and corporations would be expanded; with the increased purchasing power, their spending would rise. Stability would be restored, and the incipient rise in unemployment would be checked, as the GNP moved back to the $900 billion level. The holdings of the Stabilization Fund would either diminish or would grow at a slower rate.

The magnitude of the change required at any juncture in the surcharge increment, or in the rate of loan redemptions, would be based on the calculations of the Council of Economic Advisers, and these in turn would have to be derived from their appraisal of the business situation and from experience in the use of this new tool. But notice that errors in their calculations, while always unwelcome, would be quickly correctable. If the strength of an inflationary trend had been misjudged, or if the impact of a recession had been under- or overestimated, the volume of compulsory loan payments currently made by the public could be increased, reduced, eliminated entirely, or reversed in direction within a month, if necessary. Such errors can be, and have been disastrous under the present cumbersome system of altering, or trying to alter, tax rates or the overall volume of public expenditures.

Naturally, returning to our illustration, the stable or "full employment without inflation" level of the gross national product would not remain at $900 billion indefinitely. As the population and labor force of the nation grew, and as productivity advanced, the potential GNP consistent with full employment and stable prices would itself rise. But at any time, whether in peace or in "small" wars such as Korea or Vietnam, there would exist a target of true stability, and the tool proposed here would enable the nation to hit it consistently. Under present circumstances this achievement is not only unlikely but impossible.

A Coordinate Monetary Policy. Monetary policy could interfere with the plan just outlined, but only if Satan himself, in appropriate disguise, were to work his way into the chairmanship of the Board of Governors of the Federal Reserve System. When the President wished to counter an inflationary upsurge and imposed a substantial compulsory loan on the populace, Satan could deliberately increase the reserves of the nation's banks, and otherwise attempt to improve the liquidity of financial institutions and lower interest rates so that households and corporations might be tempted to replenish their current resources by borrowing. While the power of monetary policy is often exaggerated, it is not inconceivable that he would have some success in thwarting the President by encouraging the nation to spend more rather than less.

Similarly, if the President wished to promote business expansion by reducing surcharges and accelerating loan redemptions, a determined Satan could create formidable obstacles. The Federal Reserve, under devilish guidance, could reduce or eliminate the excess reserves of banks and engineer a substantial increase in rates of interest. The nation's money supply would become scarce in relation to its needs and expansion of employment and output would become difficult, if possible at all. Indeed, the ability of the Federal Reserve System to create mischief in this and similar ways, even without Satanic guidance, has been amply documented in impartial studies such as the notable *Standards for Guiding Monetary Policy* issued in 1968 by the Joint Economic Committee of the U.S. Congress.

The monetary policy required to implement the plan proposed here is an extraordinarily simple one, in that it would instruct the Federal Reserve simply to keep out of mischief. Its power for mischief springs from the fact that the Federal Reserve System possesses control over the nation's supply of money — defined as currency in circulation plus all outstanding demand (checking account) bank deposits. Keeping out of mischief would involve merely permitting the money supply to expand gradually and smoothly in line with the nation's long-term tendency to grow — which means at a rate of from 3 to 5 percent per annum. This elementary policy, which the Joint Economic Committee and nearly all economists today agree is the only appropriate policy for the Federal Reserve System, would allow rates of interest to find their own market level and would, in effect, keep the influence on the business situation of money and interest neutral. In this friendly environment, our three-point plan for stability could do the job for which it is intended.

᙭ Point Three: The Demise of Inflation

The two tools of stabilization already described — namely, the National Service Administration and the refundable tax program — are sufficient in themselves to maintain full employment without inflation. Nevertheless, their performance in this task, and the rate of the nation's economic growth, can both be improved if a third element is added. To explain its function we return to the illustration used above.

We had assumed, in line with the lesson of the social menu curve, that the price level was stable in the presence of a 7 percent rate of unemployment. The National Service Administration, therefore, absorbed 5 out of the total of 7 percent idle. At the same time, taxes were carefully raised to help finance the jobs and training, and, particularly, to neutralize the effect of NASAD's operation on the nation's aggregate spending. In this way, continued price stability was assured. The result was a full employment, noninflationary GNP of $900 billion, achieved, however, with some 4 million men and women engaged in the placement, training, and public employment programs of NASAD, a rather substantial number. Now the following question is raised: can a way be found for reducing the required number absorbed in NASAD programs down to a more easily manageable 2 or 3 percent of the labor force, instead of 5 percent?

An insight to the problem may be provided by a brief return to the nature of the social menu and the tendencies toward inflation that this curve reflects. Experience has shown that when unemployment is about 7 percent of the labor force, prices are stable, just as we assumed. As total spending increases and business activity is quickened, unemployment falls below this level, but prices rise. The lower the unemployment level, the faster the advance in prices. All this we have already observed, both historically and in the abstract form of the social menu curve.

Furthermore, we noted that the inflation so stubbornly characteristic of the American economy was chiefly traceable to two sets of factors that were classified as structural and psychological. If, somehow, these structural and psychological sources of inflation could be weakened, then conceivably a situation might be created in which prices would be stable in the presence of perhaps a 4 or 5 percent unemployment rate, instead of 7 percent. Then NASAD's task of maintaining full employment could be achieved by absorbing some 2 or 3 percent of the labor force (and perhaps in the longer run, only 1 percent), as opposed to the 5 percent that would be necessary under present conditions. A reduction of this kind is the objective of the third element of our program for stability.

Built-In Antidotes. One powerful blow to inflationary psychology that should not be overlooked is the mere establishment of the two institutions already described — the National Service Administration and the system of refundable taxes. For these alone would enable the government to announce that neither unemployment *nor* inflation will in the future be tolerated. The announcement itself would provide a body blow to the present tendency of all sectors of society to expect and anticipate inflation. Unions, corporations, speculators, professionals, and the rest could no longer conduct their affairs on the confident assumption that prices in general will be higher tomorrow than they are today. Accordingly, these groups would be less aggressive in attempts to hike their own prices.

In addition, a partial offset to the sources of structural inflation is provided by the training and placement services of NASAD. For one result of both of these programs would be to increase the effective supply of the skilled workers that are in most demand in the market, and more so as business expansion proceeds. It is chiefly the imbalance between demand and supply in such markets that gives rise to the "structural" increases in many wages and salaries which in turn provide the thrust of much of modern inflation.

Hence we may conclude that the first two elements of the stabilization program already described would in themselves do much to undermine the fundamental sources of inflation. The result, conceivably, could be that in our illustration the GNP might be safely allowed to expand from $900 billion to $950 billion without an advance in prices, an increase that would draw more of the labor force into private industry, leaving perhaps only 5 percent unemployed. In that case NASAD would need to absorb just 3 percent of the labor force to attain full employment. It may, however, be possible to do even better than this.

An Incomes Board. The public interest in a stable, efficient, and dynamic economy is obvious. Its deficiencies in any of these respects is soon brought home to a nation's families in their incomes, taxes, the prices they pay, and the variety and quality of the public services available. The performance of the economy can be and often has been seriously impaired by inflation. The public, judged by all accessible standards, is aware of this. The proposal of this third element of our stabilization program is that this awareness, this keen interest on the part of the public, be put to positive use for stamping out, wherever they may remain, the glowing embers of inflation.

Specifically, it is proposed that a National Incomes Board be established to reflect directly the public's interest in price stability. It would consist of a central body located in Washington together with branches and divisions around the country representative of the various geographical regions as well as industry and occupational groupings. The board is conceived *not* as a controller of prices or wages, since past experience and common sense demonstrate the futility of direct controls in a business economy. Rather, the National Incomes Board would serve as an informed national economic conscience, a negotiator and persuader, an arbitrator when called upon, a vehicle for weighing counter claims objectively, for mobilizing public opinion when special interests jeopardize the public welfare, and an adviser to other branches of government on policies related to price stability.

As a national conscience, the board along with its branches and divisions would require national representation. The central board in Washington might well consist of twelve members: three each from government, capital, labor, and consumers. Branch and divisional representation would depend upon the particular assignments. Those branches concerned with broad regions of the country such as the northeast or midwest would be constituted in the same way as the central board. Divisions concerned with particular industries such as steel or autos would have nine members: three each from capital, labor, and consumers. Divisions concerned with professional or personal service occupations such as dentists or barbers would have six members, three from the occupation and three from consumers. A technical research section would be prepared to service all boards.

The specific objectives of the National Incomes Board would be to (1) discover and disclose to the public any prices, wages, salaries, fees, or other types of income that in a pronounced and apparently unjustifiable and inflationary way get out of line with those of the rest of the country and (2) explore means for correcting such aberrations where possible. The board, including its branches and divisions, would welcome responsible complaints or other relevant information volunteered by the public. It would also, aided by its technical staff, maintain a continuing study of the nation's prices and incomes.

Terms such as "unjustifiable" and "out of line" are admittedly vague when considered abstractly, but in practice the pronounced deviations that the incomes board would seek are not so elusive. Asked the meaning of Swing, Louis Armstrong once replied, "Man, if I gotta tell you, you ain't never gonna know." The significant departures from stable, noninflationary behavior that the National Incomes Board would discourage would be equally self-evident. For example, if wages are boosted sharply for a trade in which job opportunities are declining, and unemployment is already greater than average, then that increase is both unjustifiable and inflationary. If prices in an industry are increased substantially even though costs and demand are unchanged, and unused capacity is abundant, then that increase is also unjustifiable and inflationary. If the fees of physicians and surgeons are rising spectacularly because severe, artificial obstacles bar the way for training a sufficient number of men and women as doctors, then that rise is unjustifiable and inflationary — though in this instance the fundamental cure is the difficult one of removing the stubborn obstacles.

Branch or divisional units of the National Incomes Board would intervene in such cases and wherever else they observed signs of inflationary behavior. They would confer with the parties involved, sift evidence, reach decisions, and when necessary in cases of disagreement refer disputes to the central board in Washington. When inflationary behavior persisted, despite conferences and persuasion, publicity would be used to mobilize public pressure. The National Incomes Board would also volunteer its services as arbitrator in industrial disputes. It would, in cooperation with other agencies of government, advise on countering monopolistic or other restrictive practices that tended to raise prices. For example, it would interpose the consumer's point of view, typically neglected, in the formulation of the nation's farm policy. In these, in the other ways suggested, and perhaps through channels yet to be discovered, the National Incomes Board would confront the remaining inflationary elements of the economy with rational analysis and an aroused public interest. A point that warrants emphasis is that all decisions of the National Incomes Board would be reached cooperatively, with all interested parties represented, rather than imposed by an external authority. Hence, even though unenforceable by law, the judgments on inflationary boosts in prices, wages, or other incomes would have powerful claims to the support of the public.

The reader may be reminded that this final element of the stabilization program presented here is a subordinate one. Any success that the National Incomes Board may enjoy would contribute toward reducing the net cost of the program; it would not be essential to its effective operation. Full employment without inflation, as explained earlier, can be achieved by the first two elements of the program acting alone, though at a lower level of the gross national product than might be possible otherwise. Since the future influence of a National Incomes Board cannot properly be estimated in advance, in the account of costs given below we have made the unjustly pessimistic, but conservative, assumption that the board would have no success at all, at least at the start of its operations.

𝕤 *The Net Benefits of Stability*

Estimating the gains to society of economic stability is on a par with estimating the benefits of good health. The truly important advantages in both cases elude measurement. A society without inflation is more equitable — but how to value that! Men and women freed of the fear and degradation of enforced idleness are happier — but how to value that! A nation with stable prices can trade more liberally with the rest of the world — but how to value that! Small savers and pensioners, liberated from the nightmare of rising prices, are more secure — but how to value that!

There are a few relevant measurements, however, that can be made. Arthur M. Okun, who was chairman of the Council of Economic Advisers under President Johnson, has estimated that $33 billion of output per year was lost to the United States by not maintaining full employment during the years 1958 through 1963. Okun, however, took the conventional 4 percent unemployment rate as his standard for full employment. If he had used our standard of 2 percent unemployment, the output lost per

year would have been set at about $65 billion. Both fig-
ures, of course, are rough estimates at best. They are even
rougher when used as guides to the amount of output, and
income, that would be saved for the nation in the future
if a program were adopted that guaranteed full employment without inflation. Most conservatively estimated,
however, the probable gain could hardly be fixed at less
than $50 billion per year. It could possibly be some $20
billion or $30 billion more. But notice that the conserva-
tively estimated saving of $50 billion comes to more than
one fourth of the federal government's entire budget and
to about three fourths of total military spending, including
the cost of the Vietnam war, during 1967 and 1968. The
addition to the nation's output and income, in short, would
be very substantial.

The program for stabilization presented here would
have a cost to taxpayers, naturally, but it would also yield
some highly significant savings in taxes. Our coordinated
plan would displace some seventy separate uncoordinated
job training programs now sponsored by the federal government. It would also displace a variety of other "anti-
poverty" projects and would reduce substantially the
amount of unemployment insurance benefits, public assistance, and other relief payments that are presently required. I have estimated that the gross cost of the three-
point stabilization program would be about $12 billion,
that the offsetting savings in taxes would approximate $7
billion, leaving a net cost to taxpayers of some $5 billion.
The reader may note, in comparison, that the federal government has spent some $5 billion per annum over the

last several years on space research and technology. It has also spent some $3.5 billion per annum on inflationary price supports and other subsidies for agriculture. It has provided a variety of direct and indirect subsidies, also often inflationary, for air and sea transportation, and for the petroleum and certain other industries. The lavish budget of defense authorities, *excluding* the special costs of the Vietnam war, came to $54 billion in 1968. It is just conceivable that such appropriations as these for space, agricultural, or other subsidies, and the military could be pinched a bit without perceptibly weakening the foundations of society. If the effort is made, it should be possible to come up with the $5 billion necessary for the economic stabilization program described here, with its enormous yield for the public welfare, even without an increase in taxes.

✖️ Chapter 10

Epilogue on Ideologies and Illusions

NOTHING IS SO ENDURING in the economic structure of society as the continuous necessity for change. To overlook this fundamental truth is to court a dangerous, though for some a tempting, illusion: that existing institutions can thrive, just as they are, in virtually all circumstances, in the midst of all conceivable alterations in technology, human capabilities, aspirations, and culture. For the snugly satisfied, it is a warmly comforting proposition, and it has never proved difficult to find pundits who thought they could prove it, mathematically or otherwise. Time and again in this way, Americans and others around the world have formed dangerously strong attachments to the *status quo*, portraying it, in the headier moments of history, in the roseate hues of an ideal society. The complacent "normalcy" of the 1920's was the prelude to a near revolution. The affluence of the 1950's and the 1960's, when we "never had it so good," is undoubtedly the prelude to another decade of overdue and hence exacerbated change.

For the fact, as opposed to the illusion, is that no set of economic institutions is the best, or even tolerable, for

The Welfare State

all times and all places. When a nation stagnates, impervious to the demands of its era, it invites revolution. The steadier course is to adjust institutions, deliberately and thoughtfully, to contemporary needs and pressures, with the sober realization that the requirements will be revised again in the future. Despite hampering illusions, this is the course that has, in practice, been followed in most of the West, though haltingly, and sometimes with lags that grew perilously long. It is this course, and the evolution of institutions that it entails, that transformed the classical capitalism of the nineteenth century into the welfare statism of today.

In this ceaseless evolution, the decade ahead promises to be more dynamic than most. The pressures are evident in current history — in the demonstrations and riots of the have-nots, the alienation of youth and others from the excessive materialism and cynicism of much of economic life, the unjust penalty levied on a part of society by continuous inflation, the mounting taxes that have increasingly irritated the middle class. These are the overt stimuli. Sooner or later, with more or less wisdom, under pressure that may be moderately high or nearly explosive, responses will be made.

Much of the analysis of the preceding pages has been directed toward making those responses effective. The task posed consisted first of diagnosis — unraveling the basic causes of poverty, inflation, unemployment, and the misdirected energies and resources associated with crass commercialization, concentration of economic power, and bureaucracy in business and government. The second part of the task consisted of prescription, that is, formulating the institutional changes required.

Both components required venturing beyond the conventional thinking on these subjects of the past, including the "New" Economics. Was it not the conventional thinking, and the policies such thought espoused, that had bequeathed the problems? Taking a fresh approach, our analysis led to a three-point program for achieving full employment *without* inflation, a work-welfare program aimed at rehabilitation, training, and jobs: coordination of all welfare measures into an integrated whole, and various provisions for strengthening the decision-making influence of individuals in both the public and private sectors. No grand claim is made that adoption of these proposals, in their entirety, would end all economic ills of today, much less those that will no doubt arise in the future. The problems confronted, nevertheless, are the most urgent and pervasive of our time. They will demand concrete responses, whether those suggested here or others.

The fact that change is an inescapable way of life, in economic affairs, has been acknowledged even by doctrinaire ideologists at opposite ends of the political spectrum — in practice at least, if not in theory. In the East, the blueprint of "pure" communism that inspired early founders of the Soviet Union has become more and more a curio of history. The revered principle of equal distribution of income was modified, as early as the 1930's, to permit incentive payments and other differentials reflecting differences in skills, effort, and contribution. The virtually complete centralization of economic planning, dogmatically imposed in the earlier days, has been progressively relaxed so that now even the individual plant manager can make some important decisions on his own. The labor theory of value, central to Marxist doctrine, has been qualified sufficiently to permit capital expenses and even profits to enter into the costs and prices that allocate resources. In parts of the communist world, especially Poland and Yugoslavia, the hallowed principle of public ownership of the means of production has been significantly compromised. The banning of "unearned" income has also been reinterpreted, sufficiently, for example, to permit payment of interest on savings accounts in the Soviet Union. It is not possible to tell what blueprint, what ideology, if any, communism is following today. More and more, pragmatic tests determine the acceptance or rejection of institutions. But this means more or less constant change.

In the West, the blueprint of classical capitalism ("the test of all economic decisions shall be profits," "that government governs best which governs least") is of no more consequence for current public policy than the blueprint of pure communism. In the welfare state which has evolved, government appears as an active guide and supervisor, leading consciously toward the national goals of economic stability, justice, and growth. The chief objective of this book was to devise techniques for realizing the goals more fully, as they surely will be, one way or another, sooner or later, in the future.

Viewing such changes in the East and West, a few

daring economists, including the famous Jan Tinbergen of Holland, have advanced a so-called "theory of convergence" — an hypothesis that the institutions in both parts of the world are proceeding inexorably toward some uniform model, a critical point of intersection to be reached sometime in the decades, or perhaps century, ahead. Underlying the theory is the assumption that trial and error will induce nations everywhere, in the long run, to make correct decisions, gravitating them finally to the common model: the ideal state. It is the latter concept, especially, to which many would take exception. Can we sensibly define an ideal state that would be universally recognized as such? Can we predict now the problems that will require solving, the preferences that will demand satisfaction one hundred, fifty, or even twenty years hence? The idea runs counter to the signal observation we have already made — that changing circumstances require changing social relations, and that no unique set of institutions would suffice for all times and all places, all cultures and all tastes. The ultimate destination of social evolution, if there is any such, remains indeterminable for most of us. The available facts, of course, justify the interesting observation that the economic institutions of East and West have moved significantly closer together during the past thirty years, though the distance between the two is still vast.

One paramount advantage, among certain others, lies with the West in this mutual development of economic institutions. That advantage is the flexibility of democratic political institutions. These institutions insure a com-

munication between government and the people that can
be replicated in no other way. They provide a more sensitive adjustability — a more definite promise that wrongs
will be righted, errors corrected, as the people perceive
them. The perception must be there, of course, and the
will to act upon it. The years ahead present an excellent
laboratory for testing how alert and accurate these reactions can be. There is no dearth of either errors or
wrongs that urgently command attention.

Notes to the Chapters

Chapter 1

A highly authoritative and comprehensive account of the development of economic institutions in the Western world is Dudley Dillard's *Economic Development of the North Atlantic Community*, Prentice-Hall, Englewood Cliffs, N.J., 1967. Dillard covers events from the late Middle Ages to the present. More modest, but interesting, approaches to part or all of the same material are Robert L. Heilbroner, *The Making of Economic Society*, Prentice-Hall, Englewood Cliffs, N.J., 1962, and G. D. H. Cole, *Introduction to Economic History, 1750–1950*, Macmillan & Co., London, 1954. Changes in economic institutions during the last few decades are described in Allan G. Gruchy, *Comparative Economic Systems*, Houghton Mifflin, Boston, 1966; Andrew Shonfield, *Modern Capitalism*, Oxford University Press, New York, 1965; and Neil H. Jacoby and James E. Howell, *European Economics, East and West: Convergence of Five European Countries and the United States*, World Publishing Co., Cleveland, 1967.

The reader will notice, if he consults these books or others like them, that there is very little agreement among economists on terminology in classifying economic systems. The terms socialism, welfare state, guided capitalism, modern capitalism, or just capitalism are used in a variety of ways. The particular terms employed, however, are not so important, as Dillard says on page 710 of his work. "What does matter," he adds, "is recognition of how drastically the system (of capitalism) has changed since its classical phase in the nineteenth century. The market mechanism, the mainspring of classic capitalism until World War I, has become increasingly subordinated to decisions based on the calculations of representatives of the economy as a whole. In general, this is what is meant by economic planning, and it is this trend away from laissez-faire toward economic planning which has come to prevail in most countries of the world." What is important, also, is that on such basic facts as these, virtually all economic historians are in agreement.

Chapter 2

The supposed inherent *stability* of capitalism, to which orthodox, pre-Keynesian economists were attached, is often traced back to Say's Law, the proposition that "supply creates its own demand." The prestige of this so-called law (promulgated by the early nineteenth-century French economist, Jean Baptiste Say) is amply reflected in a representative textbook of the pre-Keynesian era, Fred M. Taylor, *Principles of Economics*, Ronald, New York, 1923. Interesting discussions of the dominant attitude of economists toward stability and instability, prior to Keynes, are found in Chapter III of Lawrence R. Klein, *The Keynesian Revolution*, 2nd ed., Macmillan, New York, 1966, and Chapter VI of Seymour E. Harris (ed.), *The New Economics*, Alfred A. Knopf, New York, 1948. A neat summary of the economic theory of Karl Marx, and in particular, his rebuttal of Say's Law, is contained in Chapter 10 of Jacob Oser, *The Evolution of Economic Thought*, Harcourt, Brace & World, New York, 1963. The sunspot theory of business cycles, cited in this chapter, never attained much popularity though it was formulated by the renowned British economist, W. Stanley Jevons, who was ranked in his day as one of the four or five leading world authorities. The theory is discussed in his *Investigations in Currency and Finance,* Macmillan & Co., London, 1884.

The original source of Keynesian theory is, of course, John Maynard Keynes, *The General Theory of Employment, Interest, and Money,* Harcourt, Brace & Co., New York, 1936. The exposition of this volume, however, is not only highly technical, but curiously convoluted, so that for some years after its publication, although nearly all economists knew that it was important, they quarreled rather widely over what it meant. Since then, expositions of the theory, as well as extensions and refinements, have proliferated. Readers who wish a more detailed, but still elementary, account of Keynesian theory as it stands today, may refer to Chapters 14–18 of Melville J. Ulmer, *Economics: Theory and Practice,* 2nd ed., Houghton Mifflin, Boston, 1965, or to Chapters 11–13 and 19 of Paul A. Samuelson, *Economics,* 7th ed., McGraw-Hill, New York, 1967. Both of these books contain additional references to more extensive and technical presentations.

Chapter 3

The basic source for the data given on prices and unemployment for the various Western democracies is the United Nations' *Statistical Yearbook.* However, the figures on unemployment in foreign countries used in this chapter were in all cases inclusive of the small adjustments necessary to make them comparable with those of the United States. The statistical differences in this respect are described in the President's Committee to Appraise Employment and Unemployent Statistics, *Measuring Employment and Unemployment,* Washington, D.C., 1962. In general, because of differences in definition, the unemployment rates published by the Western European countries are slightly understated when compared with those of the United States. Unless otherwise noted, the measure of the price level used throughout this chapter has been the indexes of consumer prices, sometimes called "cost of living" indexes.

The social menu curve, as the text indicates, is a rough summary of recent experience which makes no claim to precision. Although constructed independently by the author, it compares closely, except for one significant difference, with a similar curve based on earlier data presented by Paul A. Samuelson and Robert M. Solow in "Our Menu of Policy Choices," in Arthur M. Okun (ed.), *The Battle Against Unemployment*, W. W. Norton, New York, 1965. The significant difference between their curve and mine relates to the extreme left branch, as it appears in my diagram on page 34. My curve shows that perfect stability in the price level — a zero percent annual increase — would occur in the neighborhood of a 7 percent unemployment rate. Their curve shows perfect price stability at a point slightly above a 5 percent unemployment rate. In this respect the Samuelson-Solow curve seems to be clearly in error. In every one of the years from 1958 through 1963 the unemployment rate was at, or *materially greater than,* 5.5 percent, and yet the consumer price index rose in each of the years without exception; the *average* increase for the period was about 1.5 percent per annum, even though at times the unemployment rate was as high as 7 percent. Systematic statistical investigations in this field originated with A. W. Phillips, "The Relation between Unemployment and the Rate of Change of Money Wage Rates in the United Kingdom, 1861–1957," *Economica*, November, 1958.

Note may be taken here of the contention sometimes advanced that the consumer price index, which is the usual measure of the pace of inflation, is biased upward to the tune of about 1 percent per annum, and that therefore at least a small part of the apparent inflation we have experienced over the last twenty years is merely a statistical illusion. According to this view (see, for example, Tilford Gaines, *Economic Report: The Anatomy of Inflation,* Manufacturers Hanover Trust Co., February, 1969), the *quality* of consumer goods is being constantly improved. Thus, tires now last much longer than they did some years ago, and vacuum cleaners are handier. If the quality of a good rises, let us say, by 10 percent, and if at the same time its price rises by 10 percent, the consumer is getting exactly as much for his money as he did before; in effect, the "real" price remained unchanged. So goes the argument, and it proceeds to assert that the Bureau of Labor Statistics simply records explicit price changes in the consumer price index but ignores the quality improvements that sometimes go with them. The common guess of the proponents of this view is that quality improves overall by about 1 percent per year. Hence, if the consumer price index rose by 1 percent in any year, this would "really" record perfect price stability.

I cannot accept this view. Of course, it may go without saying that I would be delighted if the ideas advanced later in this book were adopted and if as a result our economy achieved full employment along with an average advance in the consumer price index of as little as 1 percent per year. This is so vast an improvement over actual performance anywhere in the world that I would happily waive the small deviation from the ideal. But I would not venture to accept the easy reasoning above and call the result *perfect* price stability, and I do believe that a *zero* percent change in the consumer price index, on the average, is both desirable and attainable. The basis for my view is twofold. First of all, the Bureau of Labor Statistics *does* adjust the consumer price index for quality improvements. The methods used have been described fully and repeatedly by the Commissioner of Labor Statistics in the *Monthly Labor Review* and in congressional hearings (see, for example, *Government Price Statistics,* Hearings before the Subcommittee on Economic Statistics of the Joint Economic Committee, Congress of the United States, May, 1966, pp. 60–62). Whether the adjustments made by the BLS are adequate or sufficient may be arguable, but no convincing evidence of inadequacy or insufficiency has yet been presented. Secondly, it is unfortunately true that the Bureau of Labor Statistics makes no adjustment in its index, systematically, for quality deterioration — the substitution of shoddy material or workmanship, planned obsolescence, and the like. Thus, if the useful life expectancy of a commodity is reduced by one-half, while at the same time its price remains unchanged, the consumer is obviously getting less for his money and the result is therefore tantamount to a real price increase. Since adjustments for such quality reductions are ordinarily not incorporated in the consumer price index (particularly because no systematic effort is made to seek them out), there is a distinct possibility that the index, on balance, is biased downward. If this were true, of course, we would have to conclude that inflation has actually been *greater* than the official price index indicates. I say there is a *possibility* of this, an assertion that is echoed by the Commissioner of Labor Statistics in the hearings cited above, p. 61. However, in the absence of an objective study of the matter, which is sorely needed, I am more or less forced along with other mere mortals to accept the consumer price index at face value. It is all too tempting, for those who wish to excuse policy inadequacies, to say that an advance in the price index is "really" no advance at all, just as it is tempting for them to define an unemployment rate of 4 or 5 percent as "full" employment. Some economists, as well as some politicians, must learn from hard experience that Lincoln was right:

> If you once forfeit the confidence of your fellow citizens, you can never regain their respect and esteem. It is true that you may fool all the people some of the time; you can even fool some of the people all the time; but you can't fool all of the people all the time.

Walter W. Heller's testimony concerning his experience as chairman of the Council of Economic Advisers under Presidents Kennedy and Johnson is presented in his *New Dimensions of Political Economy*, W. W. Norton, New York, 1966. Some of the present writer's differences with Heller in interpreting the economic history of this period are given in my review of his book in the *Journal of Economic Issues*, March, 1968.

The data in Table 1 on the federal debt relate to the gross debt consisting of all Treasury issuances outstanding. A new measure of the federal debt was recently developed to include obligations of federal agencies, as well as the Treasury, but the new measure is available only for years subsequent to 1958. On the more comprehensive basis, the federal debt on March 31, 1969, was some $30 billion greater than the figure I give in Table 1 of the text.

Chapter 4

The 4 percent unemployment rate was officially adopted as a "reasonable and prudent full employment target for stabilization policy" in the *Economic Report of the President and the Annual Report of the Council of Economic Advisers of January 1962*, p. 46. In this and in immediately subsequent reports, the 4 percent rate was often referred to as an "interim" goal. However, the target remained officially unaltered even after it was actually achieved, and then slightly exceeded, in the late 1960's. The statement quoted on this subject by Otto Eckstein is from his essay, "Aggregate Demand and the Current Unemployment Problem," included in Arthur M. Ross (ed.), *Unemployment and the American Economy*, John Wiley & Sons, New York, 1964, p. 118. Walter W. Heller was chairman of the Council from 1961 to 1964. Robert M. Solow was a member of its staff for part of this period and Paul A. Samuelson was a consultant for all of it; both were outstanding spokesmen for the Council's point of view during the Kennedy and Johnson administrations. The attitudes of Arthur F. Burns and Henry C. Wallich toward inflation are given in their essays in *The Battle Against Unemployment*, Arthur M. Okun (ed.), W. W. Norton, New York, 1965. The differences between Burns and Samuelson are brought out clearly in their debate, published as *Full Employment, Guideposts and Economic Stability*, American Enterprise Institute for Public Policy Research, Washington, D.C., 1967.

The analysis of structural inflation presented in this chapter is essentially new; the same phrase, however, is used by Charles L. Schultze to denote a related kind of inflation in *Recent Inflation in the United States*, Study Paper No. 1, *Study of Employment, Growth and Price Levels*, Joint Economic Committee of the Congress, Washington, D.C., 1959. The use of direct price controls in Europe is described by Allan G. Gruchy, *Comparative Economic Systems*, Houghton Mifflin, Boston, 1966, and also in Mark W. Leiserson, *A Brief Interpretive Survey of Wage-Price Problems in Europe*, Study Paper No. 11, Joint Economic Committee of the Congress, Washington, D.C., December 11, 1959. The use of "guideposts" for an informal kind of direct price control in the United States was inaugurated with the *Annual Report of the Council of Economic Advisers*, January, 1962. See also *Full Employment, Guideposts and Economic Stability*, and George P. Schultz and Robert Z. Aliber (eds.), *Guildlines: Informal Controls and the Market Place*, University of Chicago Press, Chicago, 1966.

Herman P. Miller presents an interesting analysis of the changing structure of the labor force, and its effect upon the distribution of income, in *Rich Man, Poor Man*, Thomas Y. Crowell Co., New York, 1964. The quote from Walter Galenson is taken from his *A Primer on Employment and Wages*, Vintage Books, New York, 1966. The data on unemployment for different grades of labor, for youth, and for Negroes, are from *Manpower Report of the President and a Report on Manpower Requirements, Resources, Utilization, and Training,* U.S. Department of Labor, Washington, D.C., April, 1967.

Chapter 5

The data on overall expenditures for welfare by all branches of government, given early in the chapter, are from the Social Security Administration, as published in the *Social Security Bulletin,* adjusted in accord with prospective federal expenditures as provided by the Bureau of the Budget in *The Budget of the United States Government,* Washington, D.C., 1969 and 1970. The estimate of the proportion of the population in "poverty" in 1929, according to present standards, was made by the author on the basis of data on the distribution of income in that year given in *Historical Statistics of the United States: Colonial Times to 1957,* Bureau of the Census, Washington, D.C., 1950, after adjustment for price changes. Our estimate is in agreement with a similar one compiled by Eugene Smolensky in "The Past and the Present Poor," in Task Force on Economic Growth and Opportunity, *The Concept of Poverty,* Chamber of Commerce of the United States, Washington, D.C., 1965. See also the estimate of Victor R. Fuchs on the incidence of poverty in the 1930's in the same volume, p. 73. The official yardsticks on poverty are published regularly in the *Social Security Bulletin,* U.S. Department of Health, Education, and Welfare, Social Security Administration, Washington, D.C., but they are usually released with a two or three year lag. The yardsticks for 1968 used in this chapter were obtained from an updating of the Social Security data by the Treasury Department, which was released to the press on April 22, 1969. Estimates of the number of poor in recent years were taken from the Council of Economic Advisers' annual report of January, 1969.

The report on hunger in the rural south is that of the Citizens' Board of Inquiry into Hunger and Malnutrition in the United States, *Hunger, U.S.A.,* New Community Press, Washington, D.C., 1968.

Herman P. Miller's anaysis of the Bureau of the Census figures on the state of the poor is included in his essay, "Major Elements of a Research Program for the Study of Poverty," in *The Concept of Poverty,* pp. 122–3. Michael Harrington's best-known work on poverty is *The Other America: Poverty in the United States,* Macmillan, New York, 1962, and Penguin (paperback), Baltimore, 1963. Edgar May's major work in the field is *The Wasted Americans,* New American Library (paperback), 1964. Robert J. Lampman has provided succinct summaries of his voluminous works in "One Fifth of a Nation," *Challenge,* April, 1964, and "Approaches to the Reduction of Poverty: I," included in Edward C. Budd (ed.), *Inequality and Poverty: An Introduction to a Current Issue of Public Policy,* W. W. Norton, New York, 1967.

The extent of poverty among the aged, before and after social security payments, is described in the President's National Advisory Commission on Rural Poverty, *The People Left Behind,* Washington, D.C., 1967, and the U.S. Department of Health, Education, and Welfare, *Program Analysis: Income and Benefit Programs,* Washington, D.C., October, 1966. The data given on the number of aged poor, and the number of poor in other categories are taken from the excellent statistical summary given in the February, 1968, and January, 1969 annual reports of the Council of Economic Advisers.

Information on public assistance and general assistance grants by states is available from the Social Security Administration and also appears in the *Statistical Abstract of the United States,* Washington, D.C., published annually. The Joint Economic Committee material cited at the end of the chapter is from the *Report of the Joint Economic Committee, Congress of the United States, on the January 1968 Economic Report of the*

President, Washington, D.C., 1968. An interesting recent critique of some aspects of the anti-poverty program is Daniel P. Moynihan, *Maximum Feasible Misunderstanding,* Free Press, New York, 1969.

Chapter 6

Some of the landmarks in the recent, voluminous literature on guaranteed income and negative income tax plans are Robert Theobald (ed.), *The Guaranteed Income: Next Step in Economic Evolution?* Doubleday, Garden City, N.Y., 1966; essays on these subjects by James Tobin, Milton Friedman, the Ad Hoc Committee on the Triple Revolution, Harry G. Johnson, and Robert J. Lampman in Edward C. Budd (ed.), *Inequality and Poverty: An Introduction to a Current Issue of Public Policy,* W. W. Norton, New York, 1967; James Tobin, Joseph A. Pechman, and Peter M. Mieszkowski, *Is a Negative Income Tax Practical?*, Brookings Institution, Washington, D.C., 1967; Joseph A. Pechman, Henry J. Aaron, and Michael K. Taussig, *Social Security: Prospectives for Reform,* Brookings Institution, Washington, D.C., 1968; James C. Vadakin, "A Critique of the Guaranteed Annual Income," *The Public Interest,* No. 11, Spring 1968, and Chamber of Commerce of the United States, *Proceedings of the National Symposium on Guaranteed Income,* Washington, D.C., December 9, 1966. The latter presents an interesting confrontation of the largely opposing views of Robert Theobald, James Tobin, Milton Friedman, Henry Hazlitt, and Congressman Thomas B. Curtis.

Among the more carefully formulated negative income tax plans are those presented in the 1967 Brookings Institution study cited above, two of which are reproduced here in Tables 1A and 2A for reference. Both plans, as the tables show, provide a minimum income or basic allowance of $2600 for a family of four, a fairly modest standard since it is about 25 percent below the official poverty level. A family with zero earnings, in both plans, would of course receive the basic allowance in full. For other families, in the plan in Table 1A, 50 percent of earnings are deducted from the basic allowance up to the earnings level of $5200. Families with greater incomes than this would pay a positive tax. Reverting to the standards used in the body of our text, the reader will notice that the plan involves some waste, since it provides subsidies to many families above the poverty line. It also involves some impairment of work incentives, since it deducts 50 percent of earnings from the basic allowance. Despite its fairly modest standard of $2600, the cost of the plan, according to its authors, would be $26 billion.

In the second plan, in Table 2A, the *disincentive* effect on work is tempered by reducing the earnings deduction rate from 50 percent to 33⅓ percent. The predictable result, of course, is to increase waste, with subsidies going to families with earnings up to $7800. The cost of this plan, its authors estimate, is $49.3 billion.

Use of a sliding scale, instead of a flat reduction rate, would relieve work disincentives further, at least for the lower income groups, but would also result in a further increase in costs. The idea is illustrated in Table 3A. Here, deductions are arranged on a marginal basis — 10 percent on the first $1000 of earnings, 20 percent on the second $1000 of earnings, and so on up to a maximum "marginal" rate of 50 percent, as indicated in the second column of the table. Thus a family with $3000 in earnings would lose $600 of its subsidy — $100 on its first $1000 of earnings plus $200 on its second plus $300 on its third. The small total deductions at low income levels would powerfully strengthen work incentives, as compared with the other plans, but they would also, naturally, increase outlays from the treasury. The cost of the plan, at a minimum, is about $60 billion. However, the cost estimates for all the plans, and particularly for those of the Brookings Institution, may be unrealistically understated. For actual costs could substantially exceed the estimates if the work disincentives they provide induce many people to leave the labor force in favor of living on subsidies.

The full citation of the study on family income programs in foreign countries is Martin Schnitzer, *Guaranteed Minimum Income Programs Used by Governments of Selected Countries*, Paper No. 11, Materials Prepared for the Joint Economic Committee, Congress of the United States, Washington, D.C., 1968. A brief description of the Moynihan family allowance plan is

᪻ *Table 1A*

Negative Income Tax Plan of Brookings Institution, for Family of Four, with 50% Deduction Rate

Family Income before Subsidy	Net Allowance[1]	Net Income including Subsidy
0	$2600	$2600
$1000	2100	3100
2000	1600	3600
3000	1100	4100
4000	600	4600
5000	100	5100
5200[2]	0	5200

[1] The net allowance, or subsidy, is equal to the basic allowance, $2600, minus 50 percent of the family income before subsidy.
[2] At incomes above $5200, families become subject to a positive income tax.

Source: James Tobin, Joseph A. Pechman, and Peter Mieszkowski, "Is a Negative Income Tax Practical?" The Brookings Institution, Washington, D.C., 1967, pp. 4–5.

🎏 *Table 2A*

Negative Income Tax Plan of Brookings Institution, for Family of Four, with 33-1/3% Deduction Rate

Family Income before Subsidy	Net Allowance[1]	Net Income including Subsidy
0	$2600	$2600
$1000	2267	3267
2000	1934	3934
3000	1600	4600
4000	1267	5267
5000	934	5934
6000	600	6600
7000	267	7267
7800[2]	0	7800

[1] The net allowance, or subsidy, is equal to the basic allowance, $2600, minus 33⅓ percent of the family income before subsidy.
[2] At incomes above $7800, families become subject to a positive income tax.

Source: James Tobin, Joseph A. Pechman, and Peter Mieszkowski, "Is a Negative Income Tax Practical?" The Brookings Institution, Washington, D.C., 1967, pp. 4–5.

included in Sar A. Levitan, "The Pitfalls of Guaranteed Income," *The Reporter*, May 18, 1967. Moynihan's own presentation of the plan appears in the foreword he wrote for James C. Vadakin, *Children, Poverty, and Family Allowances*, Basic Books, Inc., N.Y., 1968.

🌿 *Table 3A*

Negative Income Tax Plan, for Family of Four,
with Sliding Scale Deduction Rate

Family Income before Subsidy	Marginal De- duction Rate[1]	Total De- duction[2]	Net Allow- ance[3]	Net Income including Subsidy
0	0	0	$2600	$2600
$1000	10%	$100	2500	3500
2000	20%	300	2300	4300
3000	30%	600	2000	5000
4000	40%	1000	1600	5600
5000	50%	1500	1100	6100
6000	50%	2000	600	6600
7000	50%	2500	100	7100
7200[4]	50%	2600	0	7200

[1] The marginal deduction rate is the rate of deduction applied to any excess of income above that of the preceding income bracket.

[2] The total deduction is the sum of all "marginal" deductions. Thus, for a family with income before subsidy of $4000, the total deduction is: $100 + $200 + $300 + $400 = $1000.

[3] The net allowance, or subsidy, is equal to the basic allowance, $2600, minus the total deduction.

[4] At incomes above $7200, families become subject to a positive income tax.

Chapter 7

Annual expenditures of business on advertising, with various breakdowns, are published regularly in the *Statistical Abstract of the United States*, prepared each year by the Bureau of the Census. The information on the number of dual jobholders is from *Manpower Report of the President, and a Report on Manpower Requirements, Resources, Utilization, and Training by the United States Department of Labor*, Washington, D.C., 1967. The cost of model changeovers in the automobile industry is cited in Ralph Nader, "GM and the Auto Industry: The Threat of Corporate Collectivism," *The Progressive*, September, 1968, p. 17. Harry G. Johnson's remarks on the British versus the American approach to economic life appear in his "The Economic Approach to Social Questions," *The Public Interest*, No. 12, Summer 1968, p. 76. George Meany's statement on automation is quoted in Walter Galenson, *A Primer on Employment and Wages*, Random House (Vintage edition), New York, 1966, p. 115. The projections of output and "needs" to 1975 of the National Planning Association are presented in Leonard A. Lecht, *Goals, Priorities, and Dollars: The Next Decade*, The Free Press, New York, 1966.

Wesley C. Mitchell's essay on the nature of consumer spending is reprinted in *The Backward Art of Spending Money*, McGraw-Hill, New York, 1937, Chapter 1. John Kenneth Galbraith's statement on tax increases and liberals is quoted from his *The Affluent Society*, Houghton Mifflin, Boston, 1958, rev. ed., 1969, p. 314. The report to the Joint Economic Committee on budgetary practices cited is found in Otto A. Davis, M. A. H. Dempster, and Aaron Wildavsky, "A Theory of the Budgetary Process," which appears in *The Planning-Programming-Budgeting System: Progress and Potentials*, Hearings before the Subcommittee on Economy in Government of the Joint Economic Committee, Congress of the United States, 90th Congress, 1st session, Washington, D.C., 1967. The quotation given appears on pp. 323–24. All of the figures used in this chapter on family income, national income, and government expenditures are from the U.S. Department of Commerce.

Chapter 8

I have deliberately avoided using the term "employer-of-last-resort" in this chapter or in Chapter 6, despite the fact that there is a superficial resemblance between the several proposals made in recent years under that rubric and the public employment program of the National Service Administration as set forth here. The previous proposals (such as that contained in *Technology and the American Economy,* National Commission on Technology, Automation, and Economic Progress, Washington, D.C., 1966) have been typically offered as one additional method for alleviating poverty. In the present context, on the other hand, public employment appears as a component of a many-sided, coordinated program for achieving economic stability as well as fighting poverty. The full program for economic stability is rounded out in the following chapter.

Chapter 9

It is emphasized in the illustration with which this chapter starts that maintaining price stability depends on neutralizing the expenditure-expanding impact of NASAD's operations with an appropriate increase in taxes. The formulas for determining just how much taxes would need to be increased for every dollar spent by NASAD may be found in any elementary textbook, and it did not seem interesting or useful to discuss this purely mechanical detail in the text. It may be worthwhile, however, to warn the reader that the answer is *not* the simple one of a dollar's increase in taxes for every NASAD dollar spent; some extensive calculations would be necessary. In the first place a dollar raised in taxes does not imply a $1 reduction in private spending. Typically, part of a tax increase is paid out of current saving. Hence, a $1 increase in taxes might result in a drop in spending of only 70 or 80 cents, or sometimes less. On the other hand, every dollar paid out by NASAD would not mean a full $1 increase in income for the recipient. No doubt the recipient would previously have had a small income from some other source — say, unemployment insurance or public assistance. Hence, attention would have to be focused on *net* NASAD outlays, in this sense. Furthermore, account would have to be taken of the proportions of their new incomes that NASAD employees would spend; their "marginal propensity to consume," as economists say, would be much higher than that of the other (and richer) segments of the population. In any event, the policy objective, in our example, would be to prevent any net rise, resulting from the stabilization operation, in aggregate spending in the private markets of the nation, so as to inhibit inflation. The institutional tools and mathematical formulas for doing this are simple and straightforward; the underlying arithmetic could be complicated. For fellow economists who may wish a further discussion of these and related aspects of the stabilization program, formulated along more technical lines, I have added the special note which appears on pages 193–198.

Toward the end of this chapter, the possibility is suggested that the cost of NASAD might be met in whole or in part by reducing certain other items in the federal budget. One alternative mentioned was a reduction in certain subsidies to business and agriculture. The effect of such reductions on the recipients of these subsidies would be equivalent to that of an increase in taxes and hence offer no special problem. Another alternative mentioned was a reduction in the space program, or in similar low-priority projects. A question may be raised whether reductions of the latter type might not result in unemployment. The answer is yes, but on the other hand the secondary effects of NASAD spending (generated as NASAD beneficiaries spent their new incomes on goods and services) would be to increase employment in the nation's markets, and these two forces, in the operation as a whole, would be calculated to balance one another. In any event, it is an integral part of the program for stability proposed here that overall economic activity be kept at a high level — and that would certainly mean high enough to provide ample job opportunities for the engineers, physicists, technicians, and other professional and skilled workers employed by the space agencies.

The compulsory loan, or refundable tax, program presented in this chapter is new primarily in the particular context and form in which it appears. It is presented as a technique for flexible fiscal policy, and as one element of a coordinated three-point system for economic stability. A form of compulsory lending was proposed by John Maynard Keynes and was used in Great Britain and Canada as an emergency measure during World War II to help finance the war. Both the objective and the specific form of these systems were quite different from that of the present proposal. See Walter W. Heller, "Compulsory Lending: The World War II Experience," *National Tax Journal*, June, 1951. In this section of the chapter I drew in part on a previously published article of mine, "A New Road to a Stable Economy," *The Progressive*, December, 1967.

Okun's estimate of the effect of unemployment on the GNP is taken from his essay, "The Gap between Actual and Potential Output," in Arthur M. Okun (ed.), *The Battle Against Unemployment*, W. W. Norton, New York, 1965.

The net cost of the stabilization program presented here, and discussed at the very end of this chapter, must necessarily be rough both because its required magnitude cannot be predicted precisely, and because the present expenditures of all branches of government on welfare, and therefore the possible offsetting savings, can only be estimated approximately. For the latter, I relied on the data produced by Ida C. Merriam of the Department of Health, Education, and Welfare, as published periodically in the *Social Security Bulletin*, together with the latest estimates of prospective expenditures of the Bureau of the

Budget. The *gross* expenditures for the stabilization program were based on the assumption that in the early years of its operation from 2.5 to 3 million men and women would be engaged in the various programs of NASAD at an annual cost of close to $4000 per person. The latter figure was based in part on the estimated cost of public employment given by Sar A. Levitan in "Programs in Aid of the Poor," in *Adjusting to Change, Appendix Vol. III, Technology and the American Economy*, National Commission on Technology, Automation, and Economic Progress, February, 1966, p. 39.

Chapter 10

Tinbergen's work on the theory of convergence may be found in his joint study, H. Linnemann, J. P. Pronk, and J. Tinbergen, *Convergence of Economic Systems in East and West*, Netherlands Economic Institute, Rotterdam, 1965, and in his two papers, "The Theory of the Optimum Regime," in *Selected Papers*, Amsterdam, 1959, and "The Significance of Welfare Economics for Socialism," in *On Political Economy and Econometrics, Essays in Honour of Oskar Lange*, Warsaw, 1964. Other interesting discussions of convergence appear in Carl Landauer, *Contemporary Economic Systems — A Comparative Analysis*, J. B. Lippincott Co., Philadelphia and New York, 1964; Neil H. Jacoby and James E. Howell, *European Economics, East and West: Convergence of Five European Countries and the United States*, World Publishing Co., Cleveland, 1967; Isaac Deutscher, *The Great Contest, Russia and the West*, Oxford University Press, New York, 1960; and Lynn Turgeon, *The Contrasting Economies*, Allyn and Bacon, Boston, 1963.

A Special Note
for Fellow Economists

A SIMPLE MODEL may help to illuminate some
of the technical aspects of my program for stabilization which
is presented in Chapters 8 and 9. Let us neglect frictional unemployment and also suppose that there are just two kinds of
workers in the economy, skilled and unskilled; and furthermore, that the supplies of these workers are perfectly elastic
up to their respective points of full employment, shown as
points C and A on the axes of the accompanying diagram.
Since the distances OC and OA in this diagram measure the
total amounts of skilled and unskilled potential employees in
the labor force, the rectangle OABC includes all the feasible
combinations of the two types of labor. The isoquants, U_i,
show in each case the various combinations of skilled and unskilled labor that can produce the given amount and composition of output that would be demanded at each level of
the national income. The national income is measured in physical terms, assuming prices unchanged but permitting the relative amounts of different types of goods to vary, as they typically do, with alterations in the overall level of demand. The
straight lines tangent to the isoquants, of course, are isocost
lines; their slopes measure the relative costs of skilled and unskilled labor, which it is assumed remain the same. As the con-
figuration of the isoquants indicates, it is postulated in line

The Production Function, the National Income, and Employment

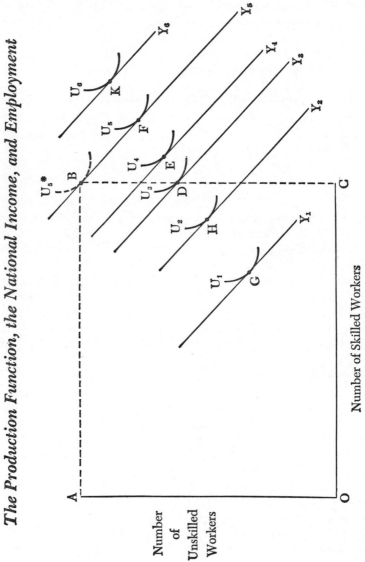

Number of Skilled Workers

with the observations made in Chapters 4 and 8 that the economy's requirements are relatively greater for skilled than for unskilled labor. In fact, as the national income rises *above* the level of Y_3 toward the nonfeasible level of Y_4, the demand for skilled labor exceeds the supply, causing inflation, although much unskilled labor still remains unemployed.

Now notice that point D denotes the highest level of output that can be achieved under the prevailing technical and cost conditions. Also, assuming that supply is perfectly elastic for both types of labor up to amounts OA and OC, which are the full employment levels of each, point D denotes the highest volume of the national income that can be reached without provoking inflation, even though, in that situation the amount DB of unskilled labor would remain unemployed. Points E and F denote situations that would arise as the money value of the national income rises *above* Y_3. Neither of these is an equilibrium position, of course, and neither could be achieved in *physical* terms, since the demand for skilled labor is in each case greater than the supply; for the same reason, both are positions of inflation. Notice, however, that in all cases the demand for unskilled labor remains *less* than the total supply, and hence there is unemployment. The isoquants are shaped to suggest a very low elasticity of substitution between unskilled and skilled labor, so that even if we were to drop the assumption of fixed relative wage rates, the situation as just described would remain approximately unchanged.

The level, Y_5, is of particular importance, because this magnitude of the national income would be sufficient to employ all unskilled as well as skilled workers at the original wage rates posited in the diagram, that is, without inflation, *if* the components of the aggregate demand of the economy were such at this level to require skilled and unskilled labor in the proportions prevailing at point B. The public employment program of NASAD, coupled with an appropriate rise in taxes called for in my plan for stabilization, are designed to alter the economy's employment requirements so as to transform the isoquant U_5 to U_5^*, thus bringing about, at point B, a noninflationary full employment equilibrium. In the longer run, the training programs of NASAD are designed to alter the relative supplies of unskilled and skilled labor, moving point C to the right and point A downward, to make possible a noninflationary full employment equilibrium at a still higher level of physical output. The compulsory loan technique is designed to provide a more sensitive and alert control over the magnitude of Y_1. The National Incomes Board is intended to reduce the pace of inflation that in practice usually sets in even before a point such as D is reached. The placement program of NASAD would also contribute to the latter end.

It may be helpful to indicate the mathematical framework of the technique for moving from undesirable positions such as H or K to the optimum at B. Let L stand for the net amount of payments into or out of the stabilization fund under the compulsory loan plan, so that when L is positive, outstanding loans on balance are being redeemed and net payments are made to the public; and when L is negative new loans on balance are being created, and net payments are made by the public to the fund. Then if $Y = C + I + G$, with all variables having their usual meanings, the consumption function would be

$$(1) \qquad C = b(Y - T + L) + C_o,$$

where b is the marginal propensity to consume, and $Y - T + L$ represents disposable income. It follows from (1) and the definition of Y that

$$(2) \qquad \Delta Y = \frac{b}{1 - b} \Delta L,$$

where $b/1 - b$ is the net loan payment multiplier. Other things being equal, then Y may be taken as a function of L, and L may be used as the chief device for moving the national income from positions such as Y_2 or Y_6 to the level of Y_5. Supposing that this has been done, the next task is to transform U_5 into U_5^*.

Let $G = G_1 + G_2$, where G_1 represents expenditures by NASAD and G_2 represents all other expenditures, and suppose that G_2 is held constant. Then it follows from the definition of Y and from (1) that

$$(3) \qquad \Delta Y_g = \frac{1}{1-b} \, \Delta G_1$$

where ΔY_g represents the increase in Y resulting from a given change in G_1. Similarly,

$$(4) \qquad \Delta Y_t = -\frac{b}{1-b} \, \Delta T,$$

where ΔY_t represents the change in Y resulting from a change in taxes. The equality

$$(5) \qquad \Delta Y_g + \Delta Y_t = 0$$

will hold when

$$(6) \qquad \Delta T = \frac{1}{b} \, \Delta G_1.$$

In other words, NASAD spending can be increased or reduced without altering the overall level of the national income, so long as taxes are simultaneously increased or reduced by an amount equal to $1/b$ times the change in NASAD spending. However, in line with our proposal, suppose that G_1 is directed exclusively, or almost so, for hiring unskilled workers, in contrast with the heavy bias toward skilled workers characteristic of the normal market demand. Then, if the proportion stated in (6) is maintained, concomitant increases in G_1 and T would transform the net composition of labor demand until, in the diagram, the equilibrium had been shifted from F to B, as desired. The size of the NASAD operation required would depend in a rather obvious way on the number of unskilled workers unemployed and the magnitude of the following parameters: the employment multiplier of G_1, the employment multiplier of $Y - G_1$, the marginal propensity to consume, and the proportion in which skilled and unskilled workers are normally demanded in the market. A further adjustment would be needed, both in the aggregate size of the operation and in the proportion stated in (6), if a significant difference were found between the marginal propensity to consume of NASAD workers and that of the rest of the nation.

Of course, only convenience in exposition dictated the complete divorce we assumed between the task of shifting Y_i, accomplished through L, and that of transforming U, accomplished through variations in G_1 and T. A variety of considerations might at times justify using other measures for part or all of the task of altering Y_i, including independent changes in G_1, G_2, or T.

Index

Aaron, Henry J., 183
Advertising, 103, 111, 116, 117, 119, 187
Agricultural price supports, 123
Alabama, 110
Aliber, Robert Z., 180
Australia, 2
Automation, 104–108
Automobile industry, 110

Balance of payments, international, 59, 118, 129–130
Banks, behavior in depressions, 22
Belgium, unemployment and inflation in, 28; and price controls, 60
Brookings Institution, 89–90, 184–186
Budd, Edward C., 182–183
Budgetary practices, 124–126
Bureau of Labor Statistics, 47, 177, 178
Burns, Arthur F., 48, 180

California, 78
Canada, 2, 100, 101; unemployment and inflation in, 28, 32
Capitalism, classical, 170; pure, and full employment, 16–18; and instability, 13–14; as idealized, 13–18; before the 1930's, 3–4; defi-

ciencies of, 7; supposed automatic stability of, 17
Census Bureau, 47, 54, 70
Churchill, Sir Winston, 66
Citizens' Board of Inquiry, 70
Classification, problems of, 1–2
Coal towns, and automation, 106
Cole, G. D. H., 173
Collective Consumption, 16
Communist countries, 11
Competition, 118; in U.S. and Europe, 104
Compulsory loans, 149–154
Connecticut, 78
Conservative government, in Great Britain, 31
Consumer price index, alleged biases in, 176–178
Consumer prices, in various countries, 28–33
Convergence, of institutions among western democracies, 2–3; theory of, 171
Council of Economic Advisers, 39–40, 48, 61–64, 69, 71, 154
Currency devaluation, 60
Curtis, Congressman Thomas B., 183

Debt, national, 41–46
Deflation, 151